T0220219

SQL on Big Data

Technology, Architecture, and Innovation

Sumit Pal

Apress®

SQL on Big Data: Technology, Architecture, and Innovation

Sumit Pal
Wilmington, Massachusetts, USA

ISBN-13 (pbk): 978-1-4842-2246-1   ISBN-13 (electronic): 978-1-4842-2247-8
DOI 10.1007/978-1-4842-2247-8

Library of Congress Control Number: 2016958437

Managing Director: Welmoed Spahr
Acquisitions Editor: Susan McDermott
Developmental Editor: Laura Berendson
Technical Reviewer: Dinesh Lokhande
Editorial Board: Steve Anglin, Pramila Balen, Laura Berendson, Aaron Black, Louise Corrigan,
     Jonathan Gennick, Robert Hutchinson, Celestin Suresh John, Nikhil Karkal,
     James Markham, Susan McDermott, Matthew Moodie, Natalie Pao, Gwenan Spearing
Coordinating Editor: Rita Fernando
Copy Editor: Michael G. Laraque
Compositor: SPi Global
Indexer: SPi Global
Cover Image: Selected by Freepik

Distributed to the book trade worldwide by Springer Science+Business Media New York, 233 Spring Street, 6th Floor, New York, NY 10013. Phone 1-800-SPRINGER, fax (201) 348-4505, e-mail orders-ny@springer-sbm.com, or visit www.springer.com. Apress Media, LLC is a California LLC and the sole member (owner) is Springer Science + Business Media Finance Inc (SSBM Finance Inc). SSBM Finance Inc is a Delaware corporation.

For information on translations, please e-mail rights@apress.com, or visit www.apress.com.

Apress and friends of ED books may be purchased in bulk for academic, corporate, or promotional use. eBook versions and licenses are also available for most titles. For more information, reference our Special Bulk Sales-eBook Licensing web page at www.apress.com/bulk-sales.

Any source code or other supplementary materials referenced by the author in this text are available to readers at www.apress.com. For detailed information about how to locate your book's source code, go to www.apress.com/source-code/.

Printed on acid-free paper

I would like to dedicate this book to everyone and everything that made me capable of writing it. I would like to dedicate it to everyone and everything that destroyed me—taught me a lesson—and everything in me that forced me to rise, keep looking ahead, and go on.
Arise! Awake! And stop not until the goal is reached!

—*Swami Vivekananda*

Success is not final, failure is not fatal: it is the courage to continue that counts.

—*Winston Churchill*

Formal education will make you a living; self-education will make you a fortune.

—*Jim Rohn*

Nothing in the world can take the place of Persistence. Talent will not; nothing is more common than unsuccessful men with talent. Genius will not; unrewarded genius is almost a proverb. Education will not; the world is full of educated derelicts. Persistence and Determination alone are omnipotent. The slogan "Press On" has solved and always will solve the problems of the human race.

—*Calvin Coolidge, 30th president of the United States*

Contents at a Glance

Contents

About the Author

 **Sumit Pal** is an independent consultant working with big data and data science. He works with multiple clients, advising them on their data architectures and providing end-to-end big data solutions, from data ingestion to data storage, data management, building data flows and data pipelines, to building analytic calculation engines and data visualization. Sumit has hands-on expertise in Java, Scala, Python, R, Spark, and NoSQL databases, especially HBase and GraphDB. He has more than 22 years of experience in the software industry across various roles, spanning companies from startups to enterprises, and holds an M.S. and B.S. in computer science.

Sumit has worked for Microsoft (SQL Server Replication Engine development team), Oracle (OLAP development team), and Verizon (big data analytics). He has extensive experience in building scalable systems across the stack, from middle tier and data tier to visualization for analytics. Sumit has significant expertise in database internals, data warehouses, dimensional modeling, and working with data scientists to implement and scale their algorithms.

Sumit has also served as Chief Architect at ModelN/LeapFrogRX, where he architected the middle tier core analytics platform with open source OLAP engine (Mondrian) on J2EE and solved some complex ETL, dimensional modeling, and performance optimization problems.

He is an avid badminton player and won a bronze medal at the Connecticut Open, 2015, in the men's single 40–49 category. After completing the book - Sumit - hiked to Mt. Everest Base Camp in Oct, 2016.

Sumit is also the author of a big data analyst training course for Experfy. He actively blogs at sumitpal.wordpress.com and speaks at big data conferences on the same topic as this book. He is also a technical reviewer on multiple topics for several technical book publishing companies.

About the Technical Reviewer

Dinesh Lokhande Distinguished Engineer, Big Data & Artificial Intelligence, Verizon Labs, is primarily focused on building platform infrastructure for big data analytics solutions across multiple domains. He has been developing products and services using Hive, Impala, Spark, NoSQL databases, real-time data processing, and Spring-based web platforms. He has been at the forefront in exploring SQL solutions that work across Hadoop, NoSQL, and other types of sources. He has a deep passion for exploring new technologies, software architecture, and developing proof of concepts to share value propositions.

Dinesh holds a B.E. in electronics and communications from the Indian Institute of Technology (IIT), Roorkee, India, and an M.B.A. from Babson College, Massachusetts.

Acknowledgments

I would like to thank Susan McDermott at Apress, who approached me to write this book while I was speaking at a conference in Chicago in November 2015. I was enthralled with the idea and took up the challenge. Thank you, Susan, for placing your trust in me and guiding me throughout this process.

I would like to express my deepest thanks to Dinesh Lokhande, my friend and former colleague, who so diligently reviewed the book and extended his immense help in creating most of the diagrams illustrating its different chapters. Thank you, Dinesh.

My heartfelt thanks to everyone on the Apress team who helped to make this book successful and bring it to market.

Thanks to everyone who has inspired, motivated, and helped me—both anonymously and in other ways—over the years to mold my career, my thought process, and my attitude to life and humanity and the general idea of happiness and well-being, doing good, and helping all in whatever little ways I can and, above all, being humble and respectful of all living beings.

Thank you to all who buy and read this book. I hope it will help you to extend your knowledge, grow professionally, and be successful in your career.

Introduction

Hadoop, the big yellow elephant that has become synonymous with big data, is here to stay. SQL (Structured Query Language), the language invented by IBM in the early 1970s, has been with us for the past 45-plus years or so. SQL is the most popular data language, and it is used by software engineers, data scientists, and business analysts and quality assurance professionals whenever they interact with data.

This book discusses the marriage of these two technologies. It consolidates SQL and the big data landscape. It provides a comprehensive overview, at a technology and architecture level, of different SQL technologies on big data tools, products, and solutions. It discusses how SQL is not just being used for structured data but also for semi-structured and streaming data. Big data tools are also rapidly evolving in the operational data space. The book discusses how SQL, which is heavily used in operational systems and operational analytics, is also being adopted by new big data tools and frameworks to expand usage of big data in these operational systems.

After laying out, in the first two chapters, the foundations of big data and SQL and why it is needed, the book delves into the meat of the related products and technologies. The book is divided into sections that deal with batch processing, interactive processing, streaming and operational processing of big data with SQL. The last chapter of the book discusses the rapid advances and new innovative products in this space that are bringing in new ideas and concepts to build newer and better products to support SQL on big data with lower latency.

The book is targeted to beginner, intermediate, and some advanced-level developers who would like a better understanding of the landscape of SQL technologies in the big data world.

Sumit can be contacted at palsumitpal@gmail.com.

CHAPTER 1

■ ■ ■

Why SQL on Big Data?

This chapter discusses the history of SQL on big data and why SQL is so essential for commoditization and adoption of big data in the enterprise. The chapter discusses how SQL on big data has evolved and where it stands today. It discusses why the current breed of relational databases cannot live up to the requirements of volume, speed, variability, and scalability of operations required for data integration and data analytics. As more and more data is becoming available on big data platforms, business analysts, business intelligence (BI) tools, and developers all must have access to it, and SQL on big data provides the best way to solve the access problem. This chapter covers the following:

- Why SQL on big data?

- SQL on big data goals

- SQL on big data landscape—commercial and open source tools

- How to choose an SQL on big data

The world is generating humongous amount of data. Figure 1-1 shows the amount of data being generated over the Internet every minute. This is just the tip of the iceberg. We do not know how much more data is generated and traverses the Internet in the deep Web.

© Sumit Pal 2016

S. Pal, *SQL on Big Data*, DOI 10.1007/978-1-4842-2247-8_1

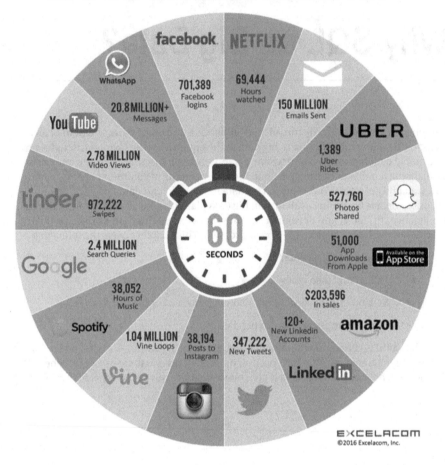

Figure 1-1. *Data generated on the Internet in a minute*

All the data generated serves no purpose, unless it is processed and used to gain insights and data-driven products based on those insights.

SQL has been the ubiquitous tool to access and manipulate data. It is no longer a tool used only by developers and database administrators and analysts. A vast number of commercial and in-house products and applications use SQL to query, manipulate, and visualize data. SQL is the de facto language for transactional and decision support systems and BI tools to access and query a variety of data sources.

Why SQL on Big Data?

Enterprise data hubs are being created with Hadoop and HDFS as a central data repository for data from various sources, including operational systems, social media, the Web, sensors, smart devices, as well as applications. Big data tools and frameworks are then used to manage and run analytics to build data-driven products and gain actionable insights from this data.[1]

Despite its power, Hadoop has remained a tool for data scientists and developers and is characterized by the following:

- Hadoop is not designed to answer analytics questions at business speed.

- Hadoop is not built to handle high-volume user concurrency.

In short, Hadoop is not consumable for business users.

With increasing adoption of big data tools by organizations, enterprises must figure out how to leverage their existing BI tools and applications to overcome challenges associated with massive data volumes, growing data diversity, and increasing information demands. Existing enterprise tools for transactional, operational, and analytics workloads struggle to deliver, suffering from slow response times, lack of agility, and an inability to handle modern data types and unpredictable workload patterns. As enterprises start to move their data to big data platforms, a plethora of SQL–on–big data technologies has emerged to solve the challenges mentioned. The "SQL on big data" movement has matured rapidly, though it is still evolving, as shown in Figure 1-2.

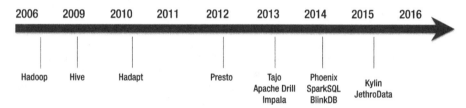

Figure 1-2. SQL tools on big data—a time line

Hadoop is designed to work with any data type—structured, unstructured, semi-structured—which makes it very flexible, but, at the same time, working with it becomes an exercise to use the lowest level APIs. This comprised a steep learning curve and makes writing simple operations very time-consuming, with voluminous amounts of code. Hadoop's architecture leads to an impedance mismatch between data storage and data access.

While unstructured and streaming data types get a lot of attention for big data workloads, a majority of enterprise applications still involve working with data that keeps their businesses and systems working for their organizational purposes, also referred to as operational data. Until a couple of years ago, Hive was the only available tool to perform SQL on Hadoop. Today, there are more than a dozen competing commercial and open source products for performing SQL on big data. Each of these tools competes on latency, performance, scalability, compatibility, deployment options, and feature sets.

---

[1]Avrilia Floratou, Umar Farooq Minhas, and Fatma Özcan, "SQL-on-Hadoop: Full Circle Back to Shared-Nothing Database Architectures," http://www.vldb.org/pvldb/vol7/p1295-floratou.pdf, 2014.

Traditionally, big data tools and technologies have mostly focused on building solutions in the analytic space, from simple BI to advanced analytics. Use of big data platforms in transactional and operational systems has been very minimal. With changes to SQL engines on Hadoop, such as Hive 0.13 and later versions supporting transactional semantics and the advent of open source products like Trafodion, and vendors such as Splice Machines, building operational systems based on big data technologies seems to be a possibility now.

SQL on big data queries fall broadly into five different categories:

- Reporting queries

- Ad hoc queries

- Iterative OLAP (OnLine Analytical Processing) queries

- Data mining queries

- Transactional queries

Why RDBMS Cannot Scale

Traditional database systems operate by reading data from disk, bringing it across an I/O (input/output) interconnect, and loading data into memory and into a CPU cache for data processing. Transaction processing applications, typically called OnLine Transactional Processing (OLTP) systems, have a data flow that involves random I/O. When data volumes are larger, with complex joins requiring multiphase processing, data movement across backplanes and I/O channels works poorly. RDBMS (Relational Database Management Systems) were initially designed for OLTP-based applications.

Data warehousing and analytics are all about data shuffling—moving data through the processing engine as efficiently as possible. Data throughput is a critical metric in such data warehouse systems. Using RDBMS designed for OLTP applications to build and architect data warehouses results in reduced performance.

Most shared memory databases, such as MySQL, PostgreSQL, and SQL Server databases, start to encounter scaling issues at terabyte size data without manual sharding. However, manual sharding is not a viable option for most organizations, as it requires a partial rewrite of every application. It also becomes a maintenance nightmare to periodically rebalance shards as they grow too large.

Shared disk database systems, such as Oracle and IBM DB2, can scale up beyond terabytes, using expensive, specialized hardware. With costs that can exceed millions per server, scaling quickly becomes cost-prohibitive for most organizations.

SQL-on-Big-Data Goals

A SQL on-big-data solution has many goals, including to do exactly the same kind of operations as in a traditional RDBMS, from an OLTP perspective or an OLAP/analytic queries perspective. This book focuses on the analytic side of SQL-on-big-data solutions, with architectural explanations for low-latency analytic queries. It also includes sections to help understand how traditional OLTP-based solutions are implemented with SQL-on-big-data solutions.

Some of the typical goals of an SQL-on-big-data solution include the following:

- *Distributed, scale-out architecture*: The idea is to support SQL on distributed architectures to scale out data storage and compute across clusters of machines. Before the advent of SQL on big data, distributed architectures for storage and to compute were far and few and extremely expensive.

  Databases such as SQLServer, MySQL, and Postgres can't scale out without the heavy coding required to manually shard and use the sharding logic at the application tier. Shared disk databases such as Oracle or IBM DB2 are too expensive to scale out, without spending millions on licensing.

- *Avoid data movement from HDFS (Hadoop Distributed File System) to external data stores*: One of the other goals of developing an SQL-on-big-data solution is to prevent data movement from the data hub (HDFS) to an external store for performing analytics. An SQL engine that could operate with the data stored in the data node to perform the computation would result in a vastly lower cost of data storage and also avoid unnecessary data movement and delays to another data store for performing analytics.

- *An alternative to expensive analytic databases and appliances*: Support low-latency scalable analytic operations on large data sets at a lower cost. Existing RDBMS engines are vertically scaled machines that reach a ceiling in performance and scalability after a certain threshold in data size. The solution was to invest in either appliances that were extremely costly MPP (Massively Parallel Processing) boxes with innovative architectures and solutions or using scalable distributed analytic databases that were efficient, based on columnar design and compression.

- *Immediate availability of ingested data*: The SQL on big data has a design goal of accessing data as it is written, directly on the storage cluster, instead of taking it out of the HDFS layer and persisting it in a different system for consumption. This can be called a "query-in-place" approach, and its benefits are significant.

  - Agility is enhanced, as consumption no longer requires schema, ETL, and metadata changes.

  - Lower operational cost and complexity result, as there is no need to maintain a separate analytic database and reduce data movement from one system to another. There is cost savings of storage, licenses, hardware, process, and people involved in the process.

- Data freshness is dramatically increased, as the data is available for querying as soon as it lands in the data hub (after initial cleansing, de-duplication, and scrubbing). Bringing SQL and BI workloads directly on the big data cluster results in a near-real-time analysis experience and faster insights.

- *High concurrency of end users*: Another goal of SQL on big data is to support SQL queries on large data sets for large number of concurrent users. Hadoop has never been very good at handling concurrent users—either for ad hoc analysis or for ELT/ETL (Extract, Load, Transform) -based workloads. Resource allocation and scheduling for these types of workloads have always been a bottleneck.

- *Low latency*: Providing low latency on ad hoc SQL queries on large data sets has always been a goal for most SQL-on-big-data engines. This becomes even more complex when velocity and variety aspects of big data are being addressed through SQL queries. Figure 1-3 shows how latency is inherently linked to our overall happiness.

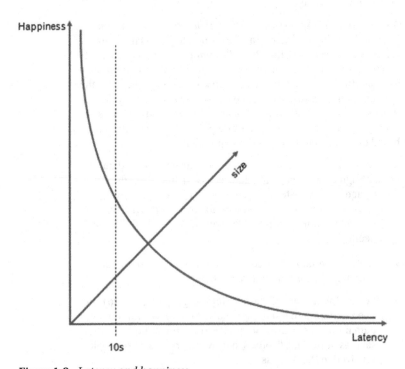

Figure 1-3. *Latency and happiness*

- *Unstructured data processing*: With the schema-on-demand approach in Hadoop, data is written to HDFS in its "native" format. Providing access to semi-structured data sets based on JSON/XML through an SQL query engine serves two purposes: it becomes a differentiator for an SQL-on-big-data product, and it also allows existing BI tools to communicate with these semi-structured data sets, using SQL.

- *Integrate—with existing BI tools*: The ability to seamlessly integrate with existing BI tools and software solutions. Use existing SQL apps and BI tools and be productive immediately, by connecting them to HDFS.

SQL-on-Big-Data Landscape

There is huge excitement and frantic activity in the field of developing SQL solutions for big data/Hadoop. A plethora of tools has been developed, either by the open source community or by commercial vendors, for making SQL available on the big data platform. This is a fiercely competitive landscape wherein each tool/vendor tries to compete on any of the given dimensions: low latency, SQL feature set, semi-structured or unstructured data handling capabilities, deployment/ease of use, reliability, fault tolerance, in-memory architecture, and so on. Each of these products and tools in the market has been innovated either with a totally new approach to solving SQL-on-big-data problems or has retrofitted some of the older ideas from the RDBMS world in the world of big data storage and computation.

However, there is one common thread that ties these tools together: they work on large data sets and are horizontally scalable.

SQL-on-big-data systems can be classified into two categories: native Hadoop-based systems and database-Hadoop hybrids, in which the idea is to integrate existing tools with the Hadoop ecosystem to perform SQL queries. Tools such as Hive belong to the first category, while tools such as Hadapt, Microsoft PolyBase, and Pivotal's HAWQ belong to the second category. These tools heavily use the in-built database query optimization techniques—a thoroughly researched area since the 1970s—and planning to schedule query fragments and directly read HDFS data into database workers for processing.

Analytic appliance-based products have developed connectors to big data storage systems, whether it is HDFS or NoSQL databases, and they work by siphoning off the data from these storage systems and perform the queries within the appliance's proprietary SQL engine.

In this section, let's look at the available products for SQL on big data—both open source and commercial.

Figure 1-4 shows some of the SQL engines and products that work on a big data platform. Tools on the right show open source products, while those on the left indicate commercial products.

Figure 1-4. SQL on Hadoop landscape

Figure 1-5 shows the same tools as in Figure 1-4 but categorized based on their architecture and usage.

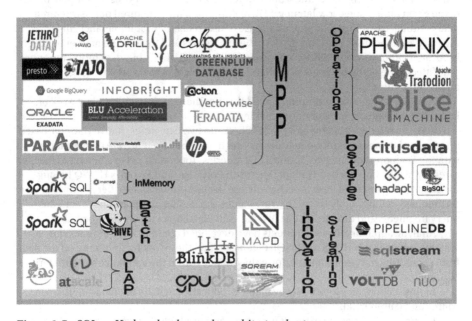

Figure 1-5. SQL on Hadoop landscape, by architectural category

Open Source Tools
Apache Drill

An open source, low-latency SQL query engine for big data for interactive SQL analytics at scale, Apache Drill has the unique ability to discover schemas on read, with data discovery and exploration capabilities on data in multiple formats residing either in flat files, HDFS, or any file system and NoSQL databases.

Apache Phoenix

This is a relational layer over HBase packaged as a client-embedded JDBC driver targeting low-latency queries over HBase. Phoenix takes SQL query, compiles it to a set of HBase scans, and coordinates running of scans and outputs JDBC result sets.

Apache Presto

An open source distributed SQL query engine for interactive analytics against a variety of data sources and sizes, Presto allows querying data in place, including Hive, Cassandra, relational databases, or even proprietary data stores. A query in Presto can combine data from multiple sources. Presto was architected for interactive ad hoc SQL analytics for large data sets.

BlinkDB

A massively parallel probabilistic query engine for interactive SQL on large data sets, BlinkDB allows users to trade off accuracy for response time within error thresholds. It runs queries on data samples and presents results annotated with meaningful error thresholds. BlinkDB uses two key ideas: (1) a framework that builds and maintains samples from original data, and (2) a dynamic sample selection at runtime, based on a query's accuracy and/or response time requirements.

Impala

Impala is an MPP-based SQL query engine that provides high-performance, low-latency SQL queries on data stored in HDFS in different file formats. Impala integrates with the Apache Hive metastore and provides a high level of integration with Hive and compatibility with the HiveQL syntax. The Impala server is a distributed engine consisting of daemon processes, such as the Impala deamon itself and the catalog service, and statestore deamons.

Hadapt

Hadapt is a cloud-optimized system offering an analytical platform for performing complex analytics on structured and unstructured data with low latency. Hadapt integrates the latest advances in relational DBMS with the Map-Reduce distributed computing framework and provides a scalable low-latency, fast analytic database. Hadapt offers rich SQL support and the ability to work with all data in one platform.

Hive

One of the first SQL engines on Hadoop, Hive was invented at Facebook in 2009–2010 and is still one of the first tools everyone learns when starting to work with Hadoop. Hive provides SQL interface to access data in HDFS. Hive has been in constant development, and new features are added in each release. Hive was originally meant to perform read-only queries in HDFS but can now perform both updates and ACID transactions on HDFS.

Kylin

Apache Kylin is an open source distributed OLAP engine providing SQL interface and multidimensional analysis on Hadoop, supporting extremely large data sets. Kylin is architected with Metadata Engine, Query Engine, Job Engine, and Storage Engine. It also includes a REST Server, to service client requests.

Tajo

Apache Tajo is a big data relational and distributed data warehouse for Hadoop. It is designed for low-latency, ad-hoc queries, to perform online aggregation and ETL on large data sets stored on HDFS. Tajo is a distributed SQL query processing engine with advanced query optimization, to provide interactive analysis on reasonable data sets. It is ANSI SQL compliant, allows access to the Hive metastore, and supports various file formats.

Spark SQL

Spark SQL allows querying structured and unstructured data within Spark, using SQL. Spark SQL can be used from within Java, Scala, Python, and R. It provides a uniform interface to access a variety of data sources and file formats, such as Hive, HBase, Cassandra, Avro, Parquet, ORC, JSON, and relational data sets. Spark SQL reuses the Hive metastore with access to existing Hive data, queries, and UDFs. Spark SQL includes a cost-based optimizer and code generation to make queries fast and scales to large data sets and complex analytic queries.

Spark SQL with Tachyon

Spark SQL can be made faster with low latency and more interactivity by using Tachyon, an in-memory file system, to store the intermediate results. This is not a product/tool by itself but an architectural pattern to solve low-latency SQL queries on massive data sets. This combination has been used heavily at Baidu to support data warehouses and ad hoc queries from BI tools.

Splice Machine

Splice Machine is a general-purpose RDBMS, a unique hybrid database that combines the advantages of SQL, the scale-out of NoSQL, and the performance of in-memory technology. As a general-purpose database platform, it allows real-time updates with transactional integrity and distributed, parallelized query execution and concurrency. It provides ANSI SQL and ACID transactions of an RDBMS on the Hadoop ecosystem.

Trafodion

Apache Trafodion is a web scale SQL-on-Hadoop solution enabling transactional or operational workloads on Hadoop. It supports distributed ACID transaction protection across multiple statements, tables, and rows. It provides performance improvements for OLTP workloads with compile-time and runtime optimizations. It provides an operational SQL engine on top of HDFS and is geared as a solution for handling operational workloads in the Hadoop ecosystem.

Commercial Tools
Actian Vector

Actian Vector is a high-performance analytic database that makes use of "Vectorized Query Execution," vector processing, and single instruction, multiple data (SIMD) to perform the same operation on multiple data simultaneously. This allows the database to reduce overhead found in traditional "tuple-at-a-time processing" and exploits data-level parallelism on modern hardware, with fast transactional updates, a scan-optimized buffer manager and I/O, and compressed column-oriented, as well as traditional relational model, row-oriented storage. Actian Vector is one of the few analytic database engines out there that uses in-chip analytics to leverage the L1, L2, and L3 caches available on most modern CPUs.

AtScale

AtScale is a high-performance OLAP server platform on Hadoop. It does not move data out of Hadoop to build analytics. It supports schema-on-demand, which allows aggregates, measures, and dimensions to be built on the fly.

Citus

A horizontally scalable database built on Postgres, Citus delivers a combination of massively parallel analytic queries, real-time reads/writes, and rich SQL expressiveness. It extends PostgreSQL to solve real-time big data challenges with a horizontally scalable architecture, combined with massive parallel query processing across highly available clusters.

Greenplum

Greenplum provides powerful analytics on petabyte scale data volumes. Greenplum is powered by the world's most advanced cost-based query optimizer, delivering high analytical query performance on large data volumes. It leverages standards-compliant SQL to support BI and reporting workloads.

HAWQ

HAWQ combines the advantages of a Pivotal analytic database with the scalability of Hadoop. It is designed to be a massively parallel SQL processing engine, optimized for analytics with full ACID transaction support. HAWQ breaks complex queries into small tasks and distributes them to query-processing units for execution.

JethroData

Jethro is an innovative index-based SQL engine that enables interactive BI on big data. It fully indexes every single column on Hadoop HDFS. Queries use the indexes to access only the data they need, instead of performing a full scan, leading to a much faster response time and lower system resources utilization. Queries can leverage multiple indexes for better performance. The more a user drills down, the faster the query runs. Jethro's architecture harnesses the power of indexes to deliver superior performance.

Query processing in Jethro runs on one or a few dedicated, higher-end hosts optimized for SQL processing, with extra memory and CPU cores and local SSD for caching. The query hosts are stateless, and new ones can be dynamically added to support additional concurrent users.

The storage layer in Jethro stores its files (e.g., indexes) in an existing Hadoop cluster. It uses a standard HDFS client (libhdfs) and is compatible with all common Hadoop distributions. Jethro only generates a light I/O load on HDFS, offloading SQL processing from Hadoop and enabling sharing of the cluster between online users and batch processing.

SQLstream

SQLstream is a platform for big data stream processing that provides interactive real-time processing of data in motion to build new real-time processing applications. SQLstream's s-Server is a fully compliant, distributed, scalable, and optimized SQL query engine for unstructured machine data streams.

VoltDB

VoltDB is an in-memory, massively parallel relational database. It falls under the category of NewSQL databases. It provides transactional capabilities and ACID (Atomicity, Consistency, Isolation, Durability) semantics of relational databases, but at a distributed scale, and provides SQL- and Java-based constructs to access the data.

Appliances and Analytic DB Engines
IBM BLU

This is a fast in-memory computing engine that works with IBM's DB2 to provide in-memory columnar processing without the limitations that require all data to be in memory for better performance. BLU's improved performance is in accelerating movement of data from storage to memory to CPU.

Microsoft PolyBase

PolyBase allows T-SQL statements to access data stored in Hadoop or Azure Storage and query in an ad hoc fashion. It allows queries on semi-structured data and can join results with data sets in SQLServer. It is optimized for data warehousing workloads and intended for analytical queries. It can work with external file formats, external data sources, and external tables. It allows T-SQL to store data from HDFS or Azure Blob as regular tables.

Netezza

Now called PureData System for Analytics, this is an appliance-based solution for analytics on large data sets. It is designed for rapid analysis of petabyte-sized data volumes. Its implementation is characterized by shared-nothing architecture, whereby the entire query is executed on the nodes, with emphasis on reducing data movement, use of commodity FPGAs to augment the CPUs, and minimize network bus traffic and embedded analytics at the storage level.

Oracle Exadata

Oracle's Exa suite of products includes Exadata, Exalytics, and Exalogic, the three classes of machines built to overcome bottlenecks in either Memory, Disk, or CPU.

> *Memory*: Exalytics is an in-memory analytics solution designed to boost performance of analytic queries typically used in BI by processing data in memory.

> *Disk*: Exadata is designed to optimize the performance of queries on large data sets, in which query overhead is experienced at the disk layer.

> *CPU*: Exalogic is designed for large application servers that require massive parallelism and scalability at the CPU layer.

13

Teradata

Originally designed as an appliance (both storage and data engine) for handling analytical queries on large data sets (way before the advent of Hadoop), Teradata is now morphing into an appliance that works with data stored in HDFS. Teradata Connector for Hadoop is a set of APIs and tools that supports high-performance parallel bidirectional data movement between Teradata and HDFS. It has an SQL engine to process queries on the data stored within Teradata or from HDFS.

Vertica

One of the first extremely successful columnar databases, Vertica is an MPP-based columnar store analytic database with the capability to run complex analytic queries with very low latency on the right hardware with the right cluster size. Vertica can integrate with HDFS as the storage layer and process data loads from HDFS.

How to Choose an SQL-on-Big-Data Solution

Owing to the surfeit of products and tools in the SQL-on-Hadoop space, it is often very difficult to choose the right one. Tool selection is not an easy task by any measure. Some of the points to consider when selecting the tools/products are listed following. This list includes questions that have to be answered by the architectural requirements, service-level agreements (SLAs), and deployment options for the tool.

- What are the latency requirements?

- What is the *fault tolerance*?

- *Deployment options*: Does the tool have to be installed across all data nodes in the cluster? Does the tool require a separate cluster? Can the tool be used on the cloud? This can have implications from budgeting, SLA, and security perspectives.

- *Hardware requirements*: Does the tool require special CPU chipsets, memory requirements, or HDD/SDD requirements?

- How does the tool handle node failures? How does the tool handle adding new nodes? How does the tool handle adding new data sets?

- *Processing requirements*: Does the tool require special processing before it can be used?

- *Analytical/SQL feature capabilities*: Not all tools are ANSI SQL compliant. Not all of them support Analytic/Window functions.

- Can the tool handle semi-structured/unstructured data?

- Can the tool handle streaming analytics with streaming data?

- *Extensibility capabilities of the tool*: How easy/difficult is it to add new features UDFs (User Defined Functions), etc., to the tool?

- *Pricing*: Some tools are priced according to the number of nodes, some by the data they ingest/work upon.

- Maturity/community size/customer feedback/number of customers

- Does it support real-time operational analytics?

- Can it perform reliable, real-time updates?

- Can it support concurrent user activity consistently with no deadlocks, etc.?

- Can it support authentication and integration with security frameworks?

- Does it provide connectivity through the drivers/APIs?

- Can it handle compressed data?

- Does it support secondary indexes?

- What kind of join algorithms does it use to speed up large joins?

- What kind of SQL Query and Query execution optimization does it offer.

Summary

In this chapter, we discussed the growth of big data adoption in the enterprise and how this has sparked a race for developing SQL-on-big-data platforms, because SQL is the most ubiquitous language used for data access in an enterprise. We discussed in detail the goals of such SQL-based solutions and the rapidly evolving landscape of tools, products, and frameworks that address the gap.

In the next chapter, we will discuss the challenges of building SQL engines for big data platforms and how to address them.

CHAPTER 2

■ ■ ■

SQL-on-Big-Data Challenges & Solutions

This chapter discusses the challenges of implementing SQL engines on big data platforms, and the possible approaches to solving them at scale and with low latency, using different techniques. The chapter introduces the SQL-on-big-data philosophy on unstructured, semi-structured, and streaming data. We will also cover the different types of SQL queries, with a focus on analytic queries.

Types of SQL

SQL is a declarative language that is highly expressive and feature-rich. There are three broad categories of SQL statements: Data Definition Language (DDL), Data Manipulation Language (DML), and Data Querying Language (DQL). The statements are used in the following ways:

- *DDL Statements*: Used to create or modify the structure/ constraints of tables and other objects in the database, including the creation of schemas and databases. When executed, it takes effect immediately. Create and Alter are examples of DDL statements.

- *DML Statements*: Used to Insert, Delete, and Update the data in the existing structures/objects in database tables. Insert, update, delete, commit, rollback, grant, and revoke are examples of DML statements. These are used to add, modify, query, or remove data from database tables.

- *DQL Statements*: Used to extract/retrieve and work with the data in the database. DQL—Data Querying—doesn't modify data in the database. SELECT <Columns> from a Table/Object is the basic example of a DQL statement.

A little more complicated and involved DQL is what are called Analytic DQL Statements or windowing queries. These queries process data on "windows"/partitions of the data, performing calculations across a set of rows related to the current row in

© Sumit Pal 2016
S. Pal, *SQL on Big Data*, DOI 10.1007/978-1-4842-2247-8_2

question. This is somewhat similar to an aggregate function; however, unlike aggregate functions, a windowing function does not return a single result for the row in question. In other words, in an analytic window query, the result set retains each individual row in the original window that was processed. The result set returns a value for every row. Let's take the simple example of a window function, to clarify the concepts.

Assume we have a data set—Employee—that has the following fields: EmpNum, DepartmentName, Salary.

If we want to find out how to compare the salary of all employees to the average salary of their department, the easiest way to do this query in SQL is to use an analytic function.

```
SELECT DepartmentName, EmpNum, Salary, avg(Salary) OVER (PARTITION BY
DepartmentName) FROM Employee;
```

The result would look something like the following:

DepartmentName	EmpNum	Salary	Avg
A	11	5200	5020.00
A	7	4200	5020.00
A	9	4500	5020.00
A	8	6000	5020.00
A	10	5200	5020.00
B	5	3500	3700.00
B	2	3900	3700.00
C	3	4800	4900.00
C	1	5000	4900.00

A window function contains an OVER clause with the function's name and arguments. The OVER clause determines how rows in the query are divided for processing by the window function. The PARTITION BY clause lists within the OVER clause how to divide the rows into groups, or partitions, that share the same values of the PARTITION BY expression. The window function basically computes the function across all the rows that fall in the same partition as the current row.

Query Workloads

Figure 2-1 shows the different categories of query workloads across the four quadrants, with the x axis showing data volumes, and the y axis showing latency. Each of the quadrants is labeled with the different query types, based on the expected latency timings and the volume of data it works with.

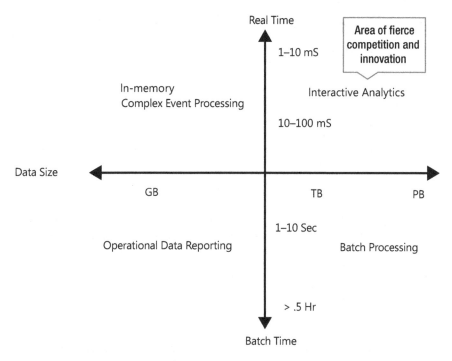

Figure 2-1. *DQL across data volumes and response time*

The lower left quadrant is where current business intelligence (BI) tools are categorized. The lower right quadrant belongs to batch tools and frameworks with large latencies. The architecture for doing SQL over batch data is discussed in Chapter 3.

The upper left quadrant represents tools and frameworks that perform complex analytics with real-time and streaming data for event processing systems—in which extreme low latencies are desirable with gigabyte-sized data sets. These systems are typically architected as in-memory solutions, whereby data is processed before it is stored; i.e., data processing occurs while the data is in motion. This requires a completely different architecture, which we will cover in Chapter 5.

The upper right quadrant represents a green playing field—a fiercely competitive zone—wherein tools and products are trying to innovate and excel and bring about newer, faster, and better solutions. Here, complex analytics queries are performed over multi-terabyte-sized data sets, with desirable latency in the hundreds of milliseconds.

Types of Data: Structured, Semi-Structured, and Unstructured

Before we start exploring the possibilities of doing SQL on big data, let's discuss the different types of data generated by Internet scale applications. Data is no longer restricted to just plain structured data. Analytics over semi-structured and unstructured data can enrich structured data and yield deeper, richer, and, sometimes, more accurate and in-depth insights into business questions. In many organizations, about 80% of the data is unstructured or semi-structured, (e.g., e-mail, document, wiki pages, etc.).

Semi-Structured Data

Any data that is not organized as a proper data structure but has associated information, such as metadata, embedded inside is called semi-structured. In semi-structured data, a schema is contained within the data and is called self-describing. Much of the data on the Web is semi-structured, such as XML, JSON, YAML and other markup languages, e-mail data, and Electronic Data Interchange (EDI).

Unstructured Data

Data not associated with structure or metadata is classified as unstructured. Textual data (e.g., e-mail, blogs, wiki posts, word and PDF documents, social media tweets) or non-textual data (e.g., images, audio, videos) are labeled as unstructured.

More often than not, unstructured data is noisy, and one major challenge of working with it is cleaning it before it can be put to use for analytics. For example, before doing Natural Language Processing (NLP) on textual data, the data has to be tokenized (i.e., stop words must be removed and stemming algorithms applied), to get it into a form in which sophisticated algorithms can be applied to make meaning out of the textual content.

Unlike SQL on structured data, SQL on semi-structured and unstructured data requires transformation to a structure that SQL Engines can interpret and operate. The acronym SQL stands for "Structured Query Language," which means it is a language that works on structured data.

Technologies such as Apache Drill and SparkSQL have evolved and are evolving further to bring the rich features of SQL to semi-structured data like JSON. You will see more in Chapter 5, in which we will discuss the architecture of SQL engines in terms of how they perform SQL over semi-structured and unstructured data.

How to Implement SQL Engines on Big Data

In this section, we will explain how SQL can be implemented at an architectural level on data sets that span across multiple machines in a Hadoop/HDFS cluster. Before we delve deeper into the architectural underpinnings of an SQL engine on Hadoop, let's look at the architectures of SQL engines on a traditional RDMS and analytics databases (MPP engine).

SQL Engines on Traditional Databases

When a SQL query is submitted to the database engine, a number of processes get to work to satisfy the query. At a high level there are two major sets of processes that spring into action: query engine and the storage engine. This is shown in Figure 2-2.

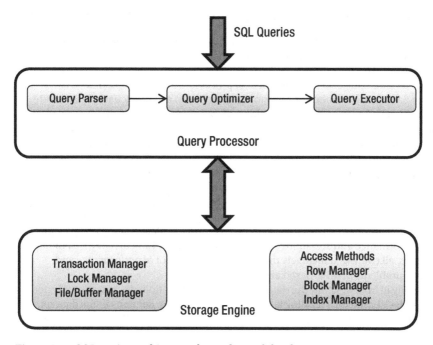

Figure 2-2. *SQL engine architecture for traditional databases*

The query engine parses the query, verifies the semantics of the query against the catalog store, and generates the logical query plan that is then optimized by the query optimizer to generate the optimal physical execution plan, based on CPU, I/O, and network costs to execute the query. The final query plan is then used by the storage engine to retrieve the underlying data from various data structures, either on disk or in memory. It is in the storage engine that processes such as Lock Manager, Index Manager, Buffer Manager, etc., get to work to fetch/update the data, as requested by the query.

Most RDBMS are SMP-based architectures. Traditional database platforms operate by reading data off disk, bringing it across an I/O interconnect, and loading it into memory for further processing. An SMP-based system consists of multiple processors, each with its own memory cache. Memory and I/O subsystems are shared by each of the processors. The SMP architecture is limited in its ability to move large amounts of data, as required in data warehousing and large-scale data processing workloads.

The major drawback of this architecture is that it moves data across backplanes and I/O channels. This does not scale and perform when large data sets are to be queried, and more so when the queries involve complex joins that require multiple phases of processing. A huge inefficiency lies in delivering large data off disk across the network and into memory for processing by the DataBase Management System (DBMS).

These data flows overwhelm shared resources such as disks, I/O buses, and memory. In order to get rid of these inefficiencies, novel indexing techniques, aggregates, and advanced partitioning schemes to limit the amount of data movement were devised over the years.

How an SQL Engine Works in an Analytic Database

Analytic databases are used in Data Warehouse (DW) and BI applications to support low-latency complex analytic queries. These databases are based on Massively Parallel Processing (MPP) architectures.

MPP systems consist of large numbers of processors loosely coupled, with each processor having its own memory and storage attached to a network backplane. MPP systems are architected to be shared-nothing, with the processor and disk operating in parallel to divide the workload. Each processor communicates with its associated local disk to access the data and perform calculations. One processor is assigned the role of master, to coordinate and collect the intermediate results and assemble the query response. A major weakness of this architecture is that it requires significant movement of data from disks to processors for executing the queries.

The interconnect between each processor-disk pair becomes the bottleneck, with data traffic adversely affecting query response timings. The inability of data transfer speeds to keep pace with growing data volumes creates a performance bottleneck that inhibits performance and scalability of the MPP architecture. Concurrency, i.e., multiple user queries, all coming at relatively the same time, causes lot of performance and scheduling problems in MPP-based architectures.

Typically in MPP systems, the data is automatically partitioned across multiple nodes (worker nodes), based on a hashing algorithm on one or more columns in the data set.

Figure 2-3 shows how a typical query would execute on an MPP system. The query first goes to the master node, where it is parsed and semantically analyzed and the query execution plan generated. The execution plan is relayed to each of the worker nodes, where some partition of the data set resides. Once the worker nodes are done executing the query in their partition of the data, results are transmitted to the master node, where a coordinator consolidates the results and returns the result set to the client.

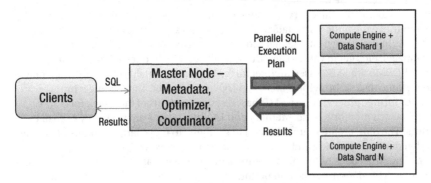

Figure 2-3. *Query execution in an MPP-based SQL engine*

Why Is DML Difficult on HDFS?

HDFS, the distributed file system on which most big data tools and frameworks are based, is architected to be WORM (write once read many). HDFS support appends but performs no updates. Modifying data becomes an inherent limitation of HDFS, hence, most SQL solutions do not support any DML operations on Hadoop. Some vendors come up with novel ways of supporting updates by logging modifications and then merging the modifications with the original data.

Challenges to Doing Low-Latency SQL on Big Data

You have experienced that relational databases do not scale beyond a certain data set size, in terms of performance and scalability. There are techniques, such as manual sharding and partitioning of data, to overcome these problems, but those, again, run into their own set of problems. One of the major challenges with distributed systems is making distributed joins perform at scale across a cluster of machines with low latency. Solving this problem runs into the inherent issues with transferring bits across the network connect at high speed and throughput.

Reducing the amount of data to be shuffled is a major challenge. Developing scalable algorithms that work with a variety of data sets, especially semi-structured data, to perform the same set of SQL functionality as on structured data is challenging, to say the least. Processing SQL queries on streaming data, in which latency requirements are more stringent and calculations require preserving state from previous computes, makes designing scalable SQL engines that work across all workloads a herculean effort. In order to work with ever-growing data set sizes, different techniques can be applied to compress and format the data with the best data layout to minimize data transfer and data access overhead.

All these challenges need to be overcome by the SQL-on-big-data engines of today and provide solutions that meet today's data-processing and querying requirements.

One of the first SQL engines on Hadoop—Hive, developed at Facebook in 2009—has some inherent limitations of doing low-latency SQL on Hadoop. This is primarily due to Hive's architecture being based on transforming SQL queries to MapReduce, and the inherent limitations of MapReduce being a batch-oriented system. Complex SQL queries require multiple MapReduce phases, with each phase writing to disk the temporary results, and the next phase reading from the disk for further processing. Data shuffling across the network, along with disk I/O, make the system slow. In the next chapter, you will see how Hive is morphing and innovating to address latency issues and overcome some of its initial architectural limitations.

MapReduce was never designed for optimized long-data pipelines, and complex SQL is inefficiently expressed as multiple MapReduce stages, which involve writing outputs from Map process to disk and then re-reading from disk by the Reduce process and data shuffling. When multiple such MapReduce stages are chained, the I/O latency overshadows the pure computation/processing latency.

Approaches to Solving SQL on Big Data

There are several categories of workloads that SQL-on-big-data solutions must address: SQL on batch-oriented workloads, SQL on interactive workloads, and SQL on streaming workloads. To add more complexity, data for each of these workloads can be structured or semi-structured.

There are basically four different approaches to doing SQL on big data:

1. Build a translation layer that translates SQL queries to equivalent MapReduce code and executes it on the cluster. Apache Hive is the best example of the batch-oriented SQL-on-Hadoop tool. It uses MapReduce and Apache Tez as an intermediate processing layer. It is used for running complex jobs, including ETL and production data "pipelines," against massive data sets. This approach will be discussed in more detail in Chapter 3. Figure 2-4 (third block) illustrates this approach.

2. Leverage existing relational engines, which incorporate all the 40-plus years of research and development in making them robust, with all the storage engine and query optimizations. An example would be to embed MySQL/Postgres inside each of the data nodes in the Hadoop cluster and build a layer within them to access data from the underlying distributed file system. This RDBMS engine is collocated with the data node, communicates with the data node to read data from the HDFS, and translates it to their own proprietary data format. Products such as Citus data and HAWQ leverage this architectural aspect of doing SQL on Hadoop. Figure 2-4 (fourth block) shows this approach.

3. Build a new query engine that co-resides in the same nodes as the data nodes and works with the data on HDFS directly to execute the SQL queries. This query engine uses a query splitter to route query fragments to one or more underlying data handlers (HDFS, HBase, relational, search index, etc.), to access and process the data.

    Apache Drill and Impala were one the first few engines in this space to perform interactive SQL queries running over data on HDFS. This category of SQL on Hadoop engines excels at executing ad hoc SQL queries and performing data exploration and data discovery and is used directly by data analysts to execute auto-generated SQL code from BI tools. This approach will be discussed in more detail in Chapter 4. Figure 2-4 (second block) illustrates this approach.

4. Use existing analytic databases (deployed on a separate cluster, different from the Hadoop cluster) that interact with the data nodes in the Hadoop cluster, using a proprietary connector to get data from HDFS, but execute the SQL queries within the analytical engine. These external analytical engines can be integrated to use metadata in Hive or HCatalog, to seamlessly work with the data in HDFS. Examples of such products include Vertica and Teradata. Figure 2-4 (first block) shows this approach.

Figure 2-4 illustrates these architectural concepts.

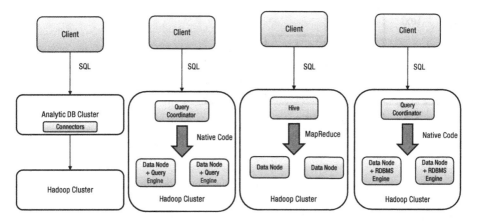

Figure 2-4. *Approaches to building SQL on Hadoop engines*

Approaches to Reduce Latency on SQL Queries

The larger the data size and larger the I/O, the longer is the time spent in scanning the data to get to the right data required to fulfill the query. Much thought, research, and innovation has gone into optimizing the storage layer to build optimizations in reducing the footprint of the data set. Below, we discuss some optimizations that can be performed at the storage layer, to reduce the I/O.

When thinking about performance improvements, there are three types of performance considerations to keep in mind:

1. Write performance—how fast the data can be written

2. Partial read performance—how fast you can read individual columns within a data set

3. Full read performance—how fast you can read every data element in a data set

File Formats

Figure 2-5 shows how data encoding can reduce data size, which eventually reduces the I/O and the amount of data a process has to scan or load in memory for processing.

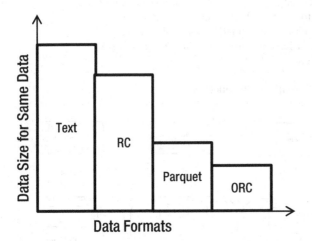

Figure 2-5. *Effect of data encoding on the data set size*

Choosing the optimal file format when working with big data is an essential driver to improve performance for query processing. There is no single file format that optimizes for all the three performance considerations mentioned above. One must understand trade-offs in order to make educated decisions. File formats can store data in a compressed columnar format. They can also store indexing and statistical information at block level.

A columnar compressed file format such as Parquet or ORC may optimize partial and full-read performance, but it does so at the expense of write performance. Conversely, uncompressed CSV files are fast to write but, owing to the lack of compression and column orientation, are slow for reads. File formats include optimizations such as skipping to blocks directly without scanning the full data and quickly searching the data at the block level.

Text/CSV Files

Comma-separated values (CSV) files do not support block compression, thus compressing a CSV file in Hadoop often comes at a significant read-performance cost. When working with Text/CSV files in Hadoop, never include header or footer lines. Each line of the file should contain a record. This means that there is no metadata stored with the CSV file. One must know how the file was written in order to make use of it. File structure is dependent on field order: new fields can only be appended at the end of records, while existing fields can never be deleted. As such, CSV files have limited support for schema evolution.

JSON Records

JSON records are different from JSON files in that each line is its own JSON datum, making the files splittable. Unlike CSV files, JSON stores metadata with the data, fully enabling schema evolution. However, as with CSV files, JSON files do not support block compression. Third-party JSON SerDe (discuss SerDe in Chapter 3) are frequently available and often solve these challenges.

Avro Format

Avro is quickly becoming the best multipurpose storage format within Hadoop. Avro format stores metadata with the data and also allows for specifying an independent schema for reading the file. Avro is the epitome of schema evolution support, because one can rename, add, delete, and change the data types of fields by defining new independent schema. Avro files are also splittable and support block compression.

Sequence Files

Sequence files store data in a binary format with a structure similar to CSV. Sequence files do not store metadata with the data, so the only schema evolution option is to append new fields. Sequence files do support block compression. Owing to the complexity of reading sequence files, they are often used only for "in flight" data, such as intermediate data storage used within a sequence of MapReduce jobs.

RC Files

Record Columnar (RC) files were the first columnar file format in Hadoop. The RC file format provides significant compression and query-performance benefits. RC files in Hive, however, **do not** support schema evolution. Writing an RC file requires more memory and computation than non-columnar file formats, and writes are generally slow.

ORC Files

Optimized RC files were invented to optimize performance in Hive and are primarily backed by Hortonworks. ORC files, however, compress better than RC files, enabling faster queries. They don't support schema evolution.

Parquet Files

As with RC and ORC, the Parquet format also allows compression and improved query-performance benefits and is generally slower to write. Unlike RC and ORC files, Parquet supports limited schema evolution. New columns can be added to an existing Parquet format. Parquet is supported by Cloudera and is optimized for Cloudera Impala. Native Parquet support is rapidly being added for the rest of the Hadoop and Spark ecosystem.

How to Choose a File Format?

Each file format is optimized by some goal. Choice of format is driven by use case, environment, and workload. Some factors to consider in deciding file format include the following:

- *Hadoop Distribution*: Note that Cloudera and Hortonworks support/favor different formats.

- *Schema Evolution*: Consider whether the structure of data evolves over time.

- *Processing Requirements*: Consider the processing load of the data and the tools to be used in processing.

- *Read/Write Requirements*: What are the read/write patterns, is it read-only, read-write, or write-only.

- *Exporting/Extraction Requirements*: Will the data be extracted from Hadoop for import into an external database engine or other platform?

- *Storage Requirements*: Is data volume a significant factor? Will you get significantly more bang for your storage through compression?

If you are storing intermediate data between MapReduce jobs, Sequence files are preferred. If query performance is most important, ORC (Hortonworks/Hive) or Parquet (Cloudera/Impala) are optimal, but note that these files take longer to create and cannot be updated.

Avro is the right choice if schema is going to change over time, but query performance will be slower than with ORC or Parquet. CSV files are excellent when extracting data from Hadoop to load into a database.

Data Compression

Most analytic workloads are I/O-bound. In order to make analytic workloads faster, one of the first things required is to reduce the I/O. Apart from data encoding, another technique to reduce I/O is compression. There are multiple compression algorithms to choose from. However, in a distributed environment, compression has an issue: compression must be splittable, so that data chunks on each data node can be processed independently of data in other nodes in the cluster.

Compression always involves trade-offs, as shown in Figure 2-6, because data must be uncompressed before it can be processed. However, systems such as Spark Succinct are being innovated to work with compressed data directly.

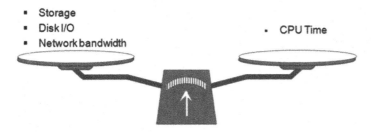

- Storage
- Disk I/O
- Network bandwidth

- CPU Time

Figure 2-6. *Compression trade-offs*

Hadoop stores large files by splitting them into blocks, hence if blocks can be independently compressed, this results in higher speedup and throughput. Snappy and LZO are commonly used compression algorithms that enable efficient block processing.

Table 2-1 shows a few of the compression algorithms and the various metrics involved.

Table 2-1. *Compression Algorithms and Their Associated Metrics*

Format	Algorithm	File Extension	Splittable	Java/Native	Compression Time	Compressed Size
GZIP	Deflate	.gz	N	Both	Medium	Low
BZIP2	Bzip2	.bz2	Y	Both	Very High	Low
LZO	LZO	.lzo	Y (when indexed)	Native	Low	Medium
Snappy	Snappy	.snappy	N	Native	Very Low	High
LZ4	LZ77	.lz4	N	Native	Low	Medium

Splittable column: This indicates whether every compressed split of the file can be processed independently of the other splits.

Native Implementations: These are always preferred, owing to speed optimizations that leverage native machine-generated code.

Figure 2-7 shows how the different compression algorithms align with each other in terms of CPU utilization and space savings.

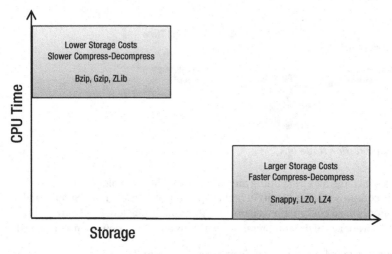

Figure 2-7. Compression algorithms trade-offs: CPU vs. Storage

Indexing, Partitioning, and Bucketing

Techniques such as indexing, partitioning, and bucketing have been tried by different vendors, to improve query latency of SQL queries. Let's take a brief look at indexing, partitioning, and bucketing in the world of big data.

Why Indexing Is Difficult

Indexing is a challenge in a world of big data that is based on a distributed file system such as HDFS. HDFS's random block placement presents difficulties in doing traditional indexes.

An index is another data file organized by one or more columns in the original raw data file. Building an index entails pointing to data in the HDFS file blocks that are randomly scattered on the distributed file system.

As newer raw data files are made available on the file system, the index somehow has to know to update itself. With traditional indexes, adding rows to a table leads to many random updates to the index files. While standard (POSIX compliant) file systems support random updates, big data storage solutions such as HDFS and S3 do not. With HDFS, existing files cannot be updated. HDFS only supports appending new data at the end of an existing file. Amazon S3 does not support random writes or file append; hence, it is impossible to implement standard indexes on HDFS or Amazon S3. When companies such as Pivotal migrated from the Greenplum database to HDFS, they eliminated index support.

JethroData, a company based in Israel, has resurrected the idea of indexes to solve some of the problems noted previously. JethroData indexes have been designed to work natively on HDFS and Amazon S3 without index update overhead. JethroData has made index maintenance so cheap that, without a second thought, every column can be automatically indexed, thus accelerating many more queries. A detailed look at JethroData architecture is done in Chapter 4.

Hive has supported indexes since version 0.8, but these are very limited in utility and not used widely. Hive supports CREATE INDEX at the DDL level. The Hive index table contains one row for each index-value, block offset and a set of block lists for each row in the block (1 = row contains the indexed column value). Hive indexes are similar to non-clustered indexes in relational databases. Hive keeps a map of the data and HDFS blocks it resides in. This enables a MapReduce job to figure out relevant blocks to process queries. Internally, Hive indexes are nothing but another file on HDFS.

The Hive DDL for creating indexes looks like the following:

```
CREATE INDEX <IndexName>
ON TABLE <TableName>(<ColumnName>)
AS 'COMPACT'
WITH DEFERRED REBUILD;
```

```
OR
```

```
CREATE INDEX <IndexName>
ON TABLE <TableName>(<ColumnName>)
AS 'BITMAP'
WITH DEFERRED REBUILD;
```

The DEFERRED REBUILD directive instructs Hive to populate the index at a later stage. When data in the base table changes, the ALTER...REBUILD command is used to bring the index up to date.

Once the index is built, Hive will create a new index table for each index, which is added to the hive metadata and can be queried/described by as any regular table.

Partitioning

Partititioning, especially in the context of Hive, allows for division of the data in a table by one or more columns, based on the values of the partitioned columns. This segregates the input records into different files/directories, based on the column values.

A simple query in Hive scans the whole table. This is a slow process, which could be speeded up by creating Hive partitions. When the table is queried, if the partitioned clause is used in the WHERE clause, only the required partitions (directory) is scanned, thereby reducing the I/O costs, by avoiding reading of data that is known not to satisfy the query, based on the partitioned column.

Advantages

- As the data is sliced in partitions across directories, a query is faster to process the partitioned part of the data, instead of doing a full scan.

Limitations

- Having too many partitions creates large numbers of files and directories in HDFS, which is an overhead to Name Node, because it must keep all metadata for the file system in memory.

- Partitions optimize queries based on WHERE clauses but are less useful for other queries not involving the partition column in the WHERE clause.

Bucketing

Bucketing is another technique used to cluster data sets into more manageable parts, to optimize query performance. It is different from partitioning in that each bucket corresponds to segments of files in HDFS. Too granular a partitioning may lead to deep and small partitions and directories that can increase the number of files and slow down Name Node performance and increase its overhead.

Bucketing can be used on tables with partitioning or without partitions. The value of the bucket column is hashed by a user-defined number into buckets. Records with the same values of the bucket column are stored in the same bucket (segment of files). Buckets help Hive to efficiently perform sampling and map side joins.

Buckets are essentially files in the leaf-level directories that correspond to records that have the same column-value hash. Hive users can specify the number of buckets per partition or per table.

When tables have been bucketed, it is important to set the number of Reduce tasks to be equal to the number of buckets. This can be done by setting the number of Reduce tasks explicitly for every job. Another way is to let Hive automatically bucket the data by setting the hive.enforce.bucketing property to true.

Recommendations

In most cases, your workloads will be bottlenecked with I/O or network. It is wise, therefore, to choose a format that reduces the amount of data that gets transferred over the wire. In most cases, it is true that CPU cores are idle while waiting to get the data and start processing. Depending on your workload pattern and the complexities of SQL analytic queries, it behooves you to choose the right data format, along with the right compression algorithm, based on whether the compression algorithm is CPU-bound or space-bound.

Always incorporate partitioning in your data ingestion and data pipelines, because that is the best way to leverage distributed systems and improve throughput. If there are too many partitions in your data, it is also advisable to consider using bucketing as a way to reduce small partitions. Partitions also help in use cases involving bad data or data quality issues or solving change-data-capture-based scenarios.

Performance tuning is a whole separate topic by itself, and performance tuning on distributed systems is an even more involved topic. A lot of performance tuning also depends on the kind of hardware, the specification of the I/O and networking, and memory sizing and bandwidth.

Summary

This chapter, we covered different types of SQL and the different SLAs associated with the different types of workloads. It also looked at the architecture of SQL engines on relational databases and how the same can be achieved with the big data-processing frameworks of today with different implementations. We discussed ways of reducing latency of SQL queries on large data sets, using different file formats, encoding, and compression techniques.

In the next chapter, we will delve deeper into the architecture of SQL on Hadoop with the Hive engine, which uses MapReduce to perform SQL queries. We will see how Hive is making architectural advances to accommodate the growing need to support low latency and reduce data-movent and shuffling issues encountered on complex MapReduce jobs.

CHAPTER 3

■ ■ ■

Batch SQL—Architecture

In this chapter, we will take a deeper look at the first SQL engine on Hadoop: Hive. We discuss the architectural details of Hive and look at how it translates SQL queries to MapReduce. This chapter also covers the recent advances in Hive that support more complex analytic and window queries and the various innovations to improve latency of SQL queries.

Hive is essentially a batch-processing system. Batch processing is a way of efficiently processing high-volume data where

> data is collected, given to the system, processed, and results produced in batches;
>
> batch jobs are configured to run without manual intervention;
>
> the system has access to all data;
>
> the system computes something complex and time-consuming;
>
> the system is generally more concerned with the throughput than the latency (latency measured in minutes or more) of the computation.

Hive

Hive was initially developed by Facebook in 2009. One of the primary reasons engineers at Facebook decided to build Hive was to enable business analysts to access the data stored in HDFS, using SQL—a language they were most familiar with. During that time, the only way to access the data stored in HDFS was to use MapReduce and Hadoop's API, which was something only seasoned developers were able to work with.

Hive is one of the first tools in the Hadoop ecosystem that most people learn to use. Hive is an SQL engine built on top of HDFS and leverages MapReduce internally. It allows querying of data stored on HDFS via HQL (Hive Query Language, a SQL-like language translated to MapReduce jobs). Hive was designed to run SQL queries as batch-processing jobs. It was not built to provide interactive querying of data on HDFS, wherein results would come back within a few seconds. However, as Hadoop began being adopted within organizations, the requirements for Hive morphed, and users started demanding more from Hive in terms of its capabilities as well as performance.

© Sumit Pal 2016
S. Pal, *SQL on Big Data*, DOI 10.1007/978-1-4842-2247-8_3

Surprisingly, however, Hive stores its metadata in a relational database, mostly either MySQL or Postgres deployed as a single instance on the Hadoop cluster. Hive supports multiple data and file formats, such as Text, SequenceFile, ORC, RCFile, Parquet, and Avro.

Hive has continually expanded its SQL capabilities by adding windowing functions, support for subqueries, and additional new data types. Hive is probably the most mature and most comprehensive SQL support structure within the Hadoop ecosystem.

Following is a list of some of Hive's most notable features:

- Hive allows applications to be written, using high-level APIs such as JDBC, ODBC, and Thrift, without writing MapReduce jobs.

- It supports external tables, which makes data processing possible without actually storing it in HDFS.

- Hive offers support for structured and semi-structured data, such as JSON and XML using SerDe.

- It supports multiple file formats, including TextFile, SequenceFile, ORC, RCFile, Avro files, Parquet, and LZO compression.

- It supports partitioning of data on different columns to improve performance.

- Hive provides complex data structure, such as Array, Struct, and Map, which facilitates working with nested, hierarchical, and semi-structured data.

- It supports enhanced aggregation and analytic functions, such as Cube, Grouping Sets, and Rollup.

- Hive offers user-defined functions (UDFs), which can be written in Python or Java.

- It supports out-of-the-box UDFs to work with XML and JSON data, such as `xpath`, `explode`, `LATERAL VIEW`, `json_tuple`, `get_json_object`, etc.

- Hive has out-of-the-box support for Text processing with UDFs.

Hive Architecture Deep Dive

Hive uses a relational store to store the metadata for all the database objects it manages. This relational store is typically either MySQL or Postgres, and it contains the metadata for all the objects: databases, database properties, tables, views, table column data types, file formats for the table, file locations, partitioning and bucketing details, etc. The metastore has a Thrift interface, whereby it can be accessed by clients written in different programming languages. Figure 3-1 depicts and overall view of the Hive architecture.

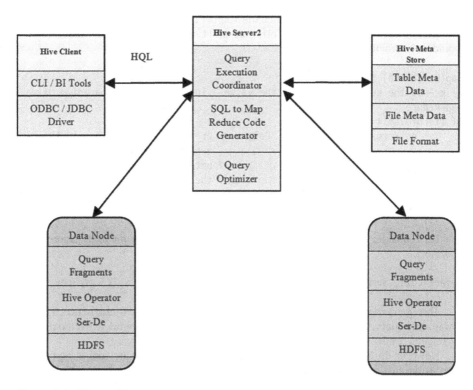

Figure 3-1. *Hive architecture*

Hive is written in Java and has an ORM (object-relational mapping) layer to read and write data into the store.

CLI, web interface, and JDBC/ODBC connectors are the various means by which clients can submit queries to Hive. Hive Driver handles query submissions and is responsible for orchestrating the life cycle of a query and managing the sessions. Each of the components shown in Figure 3-1 are discussed in more detail in later parts of this chapter.

How Hive Translates SQL into MR

In this section, we will briefly discuss how Hive Server converts an SQL query into a MapReduce program. We will offer a few examples to help you to understand the process. Note: You will require familiarity with the MapReduce framework fundamentals in order to understand this section. Let us take the most basic SQL query, such as the following:

```
Select Col1, Col2, Col3 from Table1 where Col4 = "X"
```

This query scans all the rows of a table (file in Hive), takes only those rows that have Col4 = "X", and returns the three columns—Col1, Col2, and Col3 of those filtered rows.

This query is a Map-only query, in which the Mapper code filters out the rows, based on the criterion Col4 == "X", and emits Col1, Col2, and Col3. The Map code in pseudo code would look something like this:

```
Map(k, record) {
// k - is the key and record is the value - in the key-value paradigm of
Map-Reduce
If (record.Col4 == "X") {
        outRecord = <Col1, Col2, Col3>  // Create a record with only the
                                           expected output columns
        collect(k, outRecord)           // output the collected columns with
                                           the same Key

}
}
```

Let's consider a slightly more complex query, which involves some aggregation operators.

```
Select Col1, Sum(Col2), Avg(Col3) from Table1 where Col4 = "X" groupby Col1
```

This query requires some aggregation work—Sum and Average—and, hence, it is not a Map-only query. This query would require the Reduce side framework to get the right aggregated results.

However, the Map side of this query remains very similar to the first one, except that, because we are doing a group by on Col1, the key emitted from the Map method has to have Col1 as the key. This key allows the MapReduce framework to shuffle all records with the same value of Col1 to the same reducer, which will then work on the list of records with the same values and calculate the Average and Sum of those records on Col2 and Col3.

The code for this would look like this:

```
Map(k, record)
If (record.Col4 == "X") {
        outRecord = < Col2, Col3>  // Create a record with only the expected
                                      output columns
        collect(Col1, outRecord)   // output the collected columns with the
                                      same Key

}
}
Reduce (k, listOfRecords) {
Sum = Avg = 0
foreach record in listOfRecords {
Sum += record.Col2
Avg += record.Col3
}
Avg = Avg / length(listOfRecords)
outputRecord = <Sum, Avg>
emit(k, outputRecord)
}
```

These were two very simple, basic queries translated to MapReduce. Complex queries involving joins and aggregations can often have multiple Mappers and Reducers across multiple stages, wherein each MapReduce combination feeds data through disk (HDFS) writes to the next MapReduce job in a chain before the final results are available for use.

Hive Query Compiler

Figure 3-2 shows the steps that occur inside Hive processes, from the moment an HQL is submitted until the execution is complete. This is not much different from what occurs in a typical relational database engine when an SQL query is submitted.

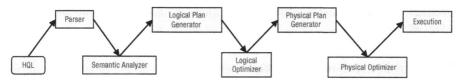

Figure 3-2. *Hive query execution*

The overall objective of the series of steps is for the Hive compiler to take a HiveQL query and translate it into one or more MapReduce jobs. The parser will parse the HQL and generate a Parse Tree, also known as an Abstract Syntax Tree (AST). The parser tokenizes the query and identifies the type of the query and the components involved in the query: table name, WHERE clause, selected columns, join type, etc. The parser also makes sure that the query is correct in terms of its syntax and structure.

The Semantic Analyzer takes the parse tree (AST) and makes sure that the query is semantically correct, in terms of validity of the objects used in the query, ensuring that the query is valid and the objects that the query refers to exist, making sure, for example, that the table referred exists. Semantic Analyzer also performs security-based authorization, from an access perspective, as to whether the given user is allowed to access the relevant objects used in the query. Metadata from the metastore is used to complete this step.

The Logical Plan Generator takes the output of the Semantic Analyzer and generates a logical plan to execute the query—in terms of what types of operators (Scan operators, Filter operators, Join operators, Select operators) would be used to satisfy the query—and builds a logical query plan that is like an inverted tree.

The Logical Optimizer takes the logical plan for executing the query and applies algorithms to optimize the query at a logical level. In other words, it applies optimizations to the logical plan with two things in mind: reducing the data scanned and improving the query latency. It does this by intelligently applying rules and using basic descriptive statistics of the existing objects to prune the data for the tables involved in the query as early as possible. This layer makes sure that whatever optimization is being done or applied will result in the same result set, without applying the optimization. This is based on the set equivalence theory.

The Physical Plan Generator takes the optimized plan generated previously and translates this to the actual implementation—in terms of what is being used as the underlying engine to satisfy the query, whether it is plain MapReduce, Tez Engine, or Spark Engine. It converts the optimized plan to operators that will actually implement the query. The transformation of an SQL query to MapReduce happens here. A complex SQL query can involve multiple MapReduce stages, and the operators to shuffle the data between the stages, etc., are added here, in this plan optimization stage.

The Physical Plan Optimizer is the final level of optimization. It applies another level of optimization, to ensure that the query uses the least amount of resources. It is here that the best algorithm to perform the join is decided—whether to apply Broadcast join or Hash join or Shuffle join or a Map Join at the implementation layer, based on the data set sizes, etc.

Finally, at the execution stage, the whole optimized plan is written to an XML file called plan.xml, which the MapReduce engine within Hive takes and submits the query to the Hadoop scheduler.

Analytic Functions in Hive

Analytic/window functions are a category of functions that are like aggregate functions but scan multiple input rows to compute their outputs. Unlike GROUP BY, which shows one result per group, analytic functions operate on groups of rows, called windows, expressed in an OVER clause as conditions.

Analytic capabilities are critical to a variety of data integration and analytic functions. Most relational databases have support for window and analytic functions in their SQL repertoire. Starting from Hive version 0.13, Hive has been steadily adding support for common analytic window functions. This allows Hive to move beyond just batch processing to a realm where it can be used to support complex analytics queries.

One minor but very important point to remember with regard to analytic functions is that they are evaluated after joins, WHERE, and GROUP BY clauses have been applied. Analytic functions are heavily used in finance and time series analytics, to provide trend, outlier, seasonality, and bucketed analysis. With the advent of IoT (Internet of Things) and streaming data, applying analytic functions on an IoT data stream becomes a very important use case.

The typical syntax of an analytic query looks as follows:

```
SELECT function() OVER ( w )
FROM ...
WINDOW w as ([ PARTITION BY ... ]
          [ ORDER BY ... ]
   [ ROWS|RANGE BETWEEN ... ]) ;
```

Following is what each clause indicates:

- PARTITION BY separates the data into distinct separable groups, similar to GROUP BY.

- ORDER BY describes how the data should be ordered within a partition.

- RANGE|ROWS BETWEEN describes which rows within the partition apply to the current calculation. The default is all the rows prior to the current one.

- WINDOW enables creation of an alias for a particular window specification, so that it can be simply referenced in multiple places within the query.

- Analytic queries enable many types of calculations that would be difficult to express with plain SQL that involves calculations across rows.

- The OVER clause is required for calls to analytic functions such as LEAD(), RANK(), and FIRST_VALUE().

- PARTITION BY is like the GROUP BY clause in the outermost block of a query. It divides rows into groups having identical values in the columns concerned. These logical groupings are known as partitions.

The following example shows an SQL pattern to generate a sequence of ID for all rows in a table. The output table has the same columns as the old one, with an additional column ID containing an increasing sequence of numbers corresponding to the order of a TIMESTAMP column in the original table.

```
CREATE TABLE EventID AS
SELECT row_number() OVER (ORDER BY date_and_time) AS id,
c1, c2, c3, c4 FROM event_table;
```

Common Real-Life Use Cases of Analytic Functions

In this section, you will see some real-life use cases of how analytic functions are being used in Hive with SQL queries.

TopN

This is used for calculating TopN queries, clickstream sessionization, and time series sliding-window analytics.

A very common use case in many SQL applications is to get the TopN rows from a table, based on some criteria. There are multiple ways to address this with plain SQL, but using window functions to partition and order, based on the criteria, and then filter the results to the desired value of N, is the most elegant and performant approach.

```
SELECT *
FROM (
    SELECT id, type, price, row_number() OVER (w)
    FROM houses
    WINDOW w as (PARTITION BY type ORDER BY price)
```

```
)  houses
WHERE row_number <= 10
ORDER BY type, price;
```

Clickstream Sessionization

Sessionization is the process of dividing a clickstream into sessions, based on key partitions, and within that partition, subdividing, based on click frequency.

What makes it interesting is that the dependency on a session is defined according to the difference between the current timestamp and the previous timestamp, which can be calculated using the lag() window function, as follows:

```
SELECT
    IP, ts,
    ts - lag(ts,1) OVER (w) > '10 minutes' as newsession
FROM clickstream
WINDOW w as (PARTITION BY IP ORDER BY ts)
ORDER BY IP, ts;
```

Grouping Sets, Cube, and Rollup

Hive has incorporated support for aggregation features for GROUP BY, using grouping sets. Grouping sets is a concise way to implement advanced multiple GROUP BY operations against the same set of data with multiple UNION and SELECT clauses.

For example, an SQL query with a grouping set looks like the following:

```
SELECT a,b, SUM(c) FROM tab1 GROUP BY a, b GROUPING SETS (a,b)
```

The preceding SQL is equivalent to the following SQL, with GROUP BY, UNION, and multiple SELECT statements:

```
SELECT a, null, SUM(c) FROM tab1 GROUP BY a
UNION
SELECT null, b, SUM(c) FROM tab1 GROUP BY b
```

The advantage of using a grouping set as opposed to multiple GROUP BY and UNION clauses is that it completes all processes in one stage of jobs, which is more efficient than GROUP BY and UNION all having multiple stages.

Hive also includes support for CUBE, and ROLLUP, based queries to be specified directly in the SQL. ROLLUP enables a SELECT statement to calculate multiple levels of aggregations across dimensions. It is an extension of the GROUP BY clause, with high efficiency and low overhead.

The ROLLUP clause is used with GROUP BY to compute the aggregate at the hierarchy levels of a dimension. GROUP BY a, b, c with ROLLUP assumes that the hierarchy is "a" drilling down to "b" drilling down to "c."

```
GROUP BY a, b, c, WITH ROLLUP is equivalent to GROUP BY a, b, c GROUPING
SETS ((a, b, c), (a, b), (a), ( ))
```

CUBE takes a specified set of grouping columns and creates aggregations for all of their possible combinations. If n columns are specified for CUBE, there will be n^2 combinations of aggregations formed.

```
GROUP BY a, b, c WITH CUBE
```

This is equivalent to the following:

```
GROUP BY a,b,c GROUPING SETS ((a,b,c),(a,b),(b,c),(a,c),(a),(b),(c),())
```

ACID Support in Hive

Now let's take a look at some of the recent additions in Hadoop and Hive to support ACID and transactions. ACID is an acronym for Atomicity, Consistency, Isolation, and Durability. ACID is what protects two people from booking the same seat in a movie theater when making an online booking.

Most NoSQL and Hadoop data stores don't support ACID. In turn, they support BASE (Basically Available Soft State and Eventual) consistency. "Basically available" means that the system guarantees availability. "Soft State" means that the state of the system may change over time, even without input that could result from the eventual consistency model.

Eventual consistency is the core concept behind BASE. Maintaining changing data in a cluster-based data-storage system that spans across data centers and is replicated across multiple locations involves latency. A change made in one data center takes a while to propagate to another data center or node. So, if two simultaneous queries are started and hit two different replicated versions of the data, they could get different answers. Eventually, though, the data will be replicated across all copies and will be consistent. This is called "eventual consistency." This is exactly what happens when, for example, you try to sell a product on Amazon. After you have successfully submitted your request to list the product for sale, Amazon's internal storage system—DynamoDB, which is an eventually consistent database—comes up with the message that it will take some time for the product to show up across different zones in Amazon's data centers.

When Hadoop was initially designed, HDFS was designed to be a WORM (write once read many times) file system. Hive provided SQL support over files in HDFS, which meant it was basically a file database platform. Starting in HDFS 2.0, data could be loaded or appended, but support for incremental updates or deletes without complex ETL (Extract, Transform, Load) -like batch transformations was not possible.

However, as of now, using Hadoop doesn't mean you have to give up on ACID. Hive now supports new SQL query syntax, which supports transactions, which has been part of relational databases since the '70s.

Some of the new SQL query syntax added to Hive include the following:

```
INSERT INTO TABLE X
  VALUES (col1, col2, ...), (col1, col2, ...);

UPDATE C SET col1 = value1 [, col2 = value2 ...] [WHERE expression]

DELETE FROM X [WHERE expression]
```

```
SHOW TRANSACTIONS;
```
Shows all currently running and aborted transactions in the system

```
SHOW LOCKS <table_name>;
```

Transaction and ACID support is very essential for multiple-use cases in the big data platform. When tracking changes made on a particular row or column over time—to determine, for example, the lineage, when they were made, and by whom—ACID becomes important. If some data was inserted inaccurately, and you want to be able to correct it, the ability to update the data becomes important.

Applications that required data merges, updates, or deletes had to rely on reinstatement of the table or partitions or buckets. Support for ACID and support for incremental updates and deletes eliminates the need to develop, maintain, and manage entire sets of complex ETL/ELT code. This provides a boost to traditional database developers to engage SQL on Hadoop, using familiar syntax and semantics, and it reduces time and effort within the development and quality analysis of operational workloads.

ACID support is essential for building transactions. Support for ACID began with version 0.13, but it was incomplete. Support for ACD (Atomicity, Consistency and Durability) was only at the partition level, and support for isolation was done using Zookeeper. Hive 0.14 introduced new APIs that completed the ACID properties' support for Hive. Transactions are supported at the row level—for Update, Insert, and Deletes.

Any change to row data is logged in row order in a file that resides in the same directory in HDFS, where the base table data resides. For each transaction or a batch of transactions, a new delta file is created. A separate directory in HDFS is maintained for the base files, and a separate one is maintained for the delta files. On read, the delta is merged into the base data, applying any update or deletes. The process of purging the delta files is known as compaction. In order to do this, all the deltas are merged into the original base file. The compaction process is done by a set of threads in the Hive metastore. During a minor compaction process, multiple delta files are coalesced into one delta file on a per-bucket basis, while for a major compaction process, one or more delta files are rewritten to a new base file on a per-bucket basis. Compaction is done both to reduce the load of too many files on the name node, as well as to reduce the latency time to merge on the fly while processing the query. Compactions are generally scheduled by the Thrift server, and the only way for an end user to run compactions is by using the ALTER TABLE COMPACT command. The compactor is clever enough not to remove a delta file until all the readers have finished their reads.

However, there are constraints to supporting transactions in Hive. Only ORC formats can support transactions, and tables have to be bucketed to support transactions. Transactional statements such as BEGIN, COMMIT, and ROLLBACK are not yet supported, and all operations are automatically committed. Transaction support is off by default. From an isolation perspective, only the snapshot isolation level is supported. Other isolation levels, such as read committed, repeatable read, and serializable, are not supported as of now. A reader will see consistent data for the duration of the query.

In order to provide the durability feature of transaction, all transaction-related metadata is stored in the Hive metastore. A new lock manager has been added to Hive, to support transactions. All lock metadata is stored in the Hive metastore. To ensure that no lock or transaction is left in the state of limbo, a keep alive, or heartbeat, mechanism has been implemented, whereby each lock holder and transaction communicates with the metastore to indicate liveliness.

The following properties have to be set in order to support transactions:

- `hive.support.concurrency`—true
- `hive.enforce.bucketing`— true
- `hive.exec.dynamic.partition.mode`—nonstrict
- `hive.txn.manager`—org.apache.hadoop.hive.ql.lockmgr.
  DbTxnManager
- `hive.compactor.initiator.on`—true
- `hive.compactor.worker.threads`—must be set to at least 1 for
  the Thrift metastore service.

When creating a table that supports a transaction, the following clauses need to be used: `buckets`, `ORC`, and `TBLPROPERTIES`, as follows:

```
CREATE TABLE Users(Name string, Address string, Designation string)
clustered by (Name) into 10 buckets stored as orc TBLPROPERTIES
('transactional'='true');
```

However, Update is not supported on the column on which the table is bucketed. Typically, this feature in Hive should be used only for data warehousing applications and not for OLTP-based applications.

As a part of Hadoop's new API changes to support ACID, a new input format called `AcidInputFormat` has been added. This class and its associated methods allow external applications to write into Hive, using ACID semantics.

Examples of such applications can include streaming applications and data warehousing applications that update dimension tables and fact table insert and updates. This API only supports batch updates, and not simultaneous updates, as replacements for OLTP applications. Each operation writes to a new delta directory, which is created when events insert, update, or delete rows. Files are stored and sorted by the original transaction id, bucket id, and row id, and current transaction id, which is modifying the row in question.

Serialization and SerDe in Hive

Hive has capabilities built in for extensibility, to interact with different data formats and to allow an end user to plug in new functionality for data transformations using UDFs (user-defined functions), UDTFs (user-defined table functions) and UDAFs (user-defined aggregate functions). We will not be discussing the details of UDFs, UDTFs, and UDAFs here but will take a look at the concept of SerDe.

Serialization is the process of converting raw data into a byte stream, which is transmitted through the network, and for storage. Serialization is very important within the Hadoop ecosystem, because it reduces the data footprint, resulting in lesser storage and faster data transfer. Extensibility components such as SerDe and ObjectInspector interfaces provide Hive the capability to integrate with different data types and legacy data.

Serialization is the conversion of structured data into its raw form, while deserialization is the process of reconstructing structured form from the raw byte stream. Deserialization allows Hive to read data from a table, and serialization is writing it into HDFS. Hive has a number of built-in SerDe classes, and it supports building new custom serializers and deserializers for your own use case.

Hive was originally built to work with MapReduce's file format, such as SequenceFile format and TextFormat. The whole idea of moving to the ORC file format was conceived to reduce I/O by reading only relevant columns, as required by the query, and supporting efficient columnar compression.

Before we go on to the next part, a brief comment on some of terms such as InputFormat and OutputFormat is worth providing. InputFormat defines how to read data from a raw input file into the Mapper. Because raw data can be in any format, InputFormat conveys the file format to the Mapper object. Typical InputFormats would be TextInputFormat, KeyValueTextInputFormat, NLineInputFormat, and so on.

The output side follows a similar concept, called OutputFormat, which defines to the Reducer process how to output the data.

Any record read by the InputFormat class in Hive is converted by the deserializer to a Java object, and an ObjectInspector converts this Java object to Hive's internal type system. By default, when no InputFormat, OutputFormat, or SerDe is specified, Hive reverts to using a built-in SerDe class called LazySimpleSerDe. The ObjectInspector is the glue of the data types in Hive with the file formats. Hive has a multitude of ObjectInspectors to support Java primitives and collections of Java objects. Figure 3-3 shows how the SerDe mechanism fits in the large scheme of things with respect to ObjectInspector and InputFormats and RecordReaders.

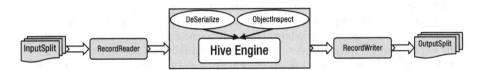

Figure 3-3. *Hive deserialization internals*

The entire SerDe mechanism in Hive is an extensible and flexible way to allow Hive to work with any file format. If one wanted to make Hive work with an unknown format that is still not invented, writing a SerDe for that format would provide an easy way to integrate Hive with that data format.

Let's take an example of how to work with JSON data in a Hive table using JSON SerDe. If we have a file with JSON data as the following:

```
{"Country":"A","Languages":["L1","L2","L3"],"Geography":{"Lat":"Lat1", "Long
":"Long1"},"Demographics":{"Male":"10000", "Female":"12000"}}
```

Let us create a Hive table using JSON SerDe to work with the JSON data in the preceding file.

The Hive DDL would look like

```
CREATE TABLE JSonExample (
        Country string,
        Languages array<string>,
        Geography map<string,string>,
        Demographics map<string,int>
        )
ROW FORMAT SERDE 'org.openx.data.jsonserde.JsonSerDe'
STORED AS TEXTFILE;
```

Here, we are using the JSON from openx. Once the table is defined and data is loaded using

```
LOAD DATA LOCAL INPATH 'json_data_file.txt' OVERWRITE INTO TABLE
JSonExample;
```

one can run SQL queries on the preceding table, using the following queries:

```
Select Country from JSonExample; // Will return "A"
Select Languages[0] from JSonExample; // Will return "L1"
Select Languages from JSonExample; // Will return ["L1", "L2", "L3"]
Select Geography["Lat"] from JSonExample; // Will return "Lat1"
```

Although at the highest level, we are using SQL under the hood, the Hive engine is using SerDe to read the data from the file, parsing it, and passing objects to the Hive Java code, to run the MapReduce job to get the results.

Performance Improvements in Hive

Over the last few releases of Hive, starting from version 0.10, Hive has gone through multiple changes, focused primarily on improving the performance of SQL queries. Some of these changes have resulted in 100–150x speed improvements. Hive was originally built around a one-size-fits-all MapReduce execution framework that was optimized for batch execution. While this solution worked for some workloads and applications, it turned out to be inefficient for many types of workloads, especially where multiple MapReduce jobs were chained or for machine learning algorithms that required iterative data processing.

Apache Tez, a new engine that works closely with YARN, generalizes the MapReduce paradigm with a framework based on expressing computations as a dataflow graph. Tez is not meant directly for end users, but it enables developers to build end-user applications with much better performance and flexibility. Tez helps Hive to support both interactive and batch queries by reducing the latency.

Hive has a setting

```
set hive.execution.engine=tez;
```

that specifies the type of engine Hive should use to execute the SQL queries. By default, Hive will revert to using plain MapReduce with no optimization. If set to Tez, Hive will use the Tez engine, which will result in queries executing faster, in most cases.

The following sections offer a deeper look at some of those optimizations. Some of the goals of Tez are to allow for low latency on interactive queries and improve the throughput for batch queries. Tez optimizes Hive jobs by eliminating synchronization barriers and minimization of the reads and write to HDFS.

Some of these changes include vectorization of queries, ORC columnar format support, use of a cost-based optimizer (CBO), and incorporation of LLAP (Live Long and Process) functionality. Pipelined execution of the reducer without writing intermediate results to disk, vectorized query execution, and other novel approaches (some of which are discussed later in this chapter) for query execution fall outside the scope and capabilities of the pure MapReduce framework.

Startup costs of Java virtual machines (JVMs) have always been the key bottleneck in Hive, where each JVM started for each mapper/reducer can often take up to 100ms or so.

Let's look at a simple Select query with a group by clause.

```
Select Table1.col1, Table1.Average, Table2.Count From (select col1,
avg(col2) from X group by col1) Table1 Join (select col1, count(col2) from Y
group by col1) Table2 On (Table1.col1 = Table2.col2)
```

Figure 3-4 shows the logical plan of how each section of the query is translated to map and reduce tasks and how the intermediate results of the map or reduce is written to HDFS before being used by the next section.

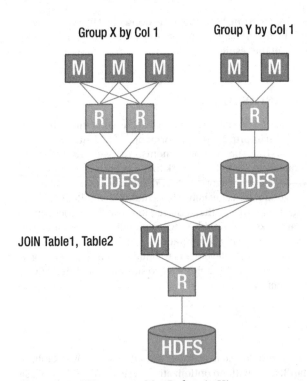

Figure 3-4. *SQL query to MapReduce in Hive*

Figure 3-5 shows how the Tez engine eliminates the extra disk write (by Map Tasks) and reads (Reduce Tasks) from HDFS. This optimization itself results in better throughput and lower latency, because the disk access is eliminated.

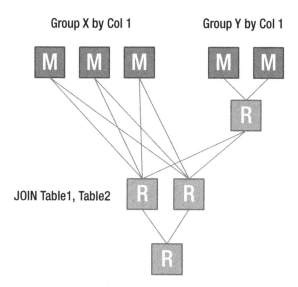

Figure 3-5. *Same SQL query, with the Tez execution engine*

Optimization by Using a Broadcast Join

Let's consider a simple SQL query with no aggregation and involving a relatively smaller table in the right-hand side of the JOIN clause (Inventory Table).

```
SELECT sales.item, sales.quantity,inventory.quantityleft
FROM sales JOIN inventory
ON (sales.productId = inventory.productID)
```

Without Tez, the SQL query would be executed using the MapReduce data flow, as in Figure 3-6, with temporary writes to disk.

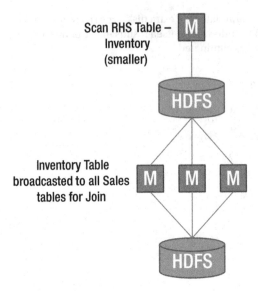

Figure 3-6. *Hive query execution without the Tez engine, with Inventory Table broadcasted to all Sales tables*

However, with the optimizations by the Tez engine, the same SQL query is executed efficiently, by broadcasting the smaller table to all the mapper tasks in the next stage, and there are no intermediate writes to disk (see Figure 3-7).

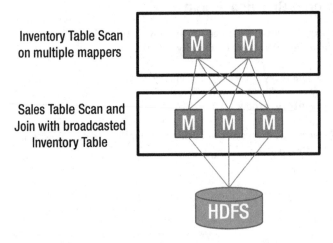

Figure 3-7. *Hive query execution with the Tez engine*

Let's take another SQL query, with aggregation and group by clause, that involves a relatively smaller table at the right-hand side of the JOIN clause.

```
SELECT SalesTable.item, SalesTable.quantity, SalesTable.AvgPrice, inventory.
quantityLeft
FROM (select item, quantity, avg(sales.sellPrice) as AvgPrice,  FROM Sales
GROUPBY item, quantity) SalesTable
JOIN Inventory
ON (sales.itemId = inventory.itemID)
```

Without Tez, the SQL query would be executed using the MapReduce code, as shown in Figure 3-8, with temporary writes to disk.

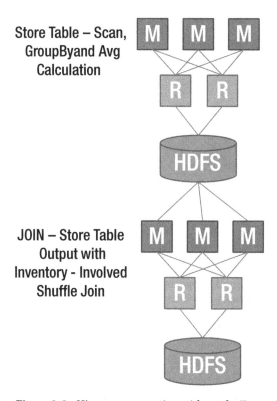

Figure 3-8. *Hive query execution without the Tez engine*

However, with the optimizations by the Tez engine, the same SQL query is executed efficiently, by broadcasting the smaller table to all the mapper tasks in the next stage, and there are no intermediate writes to disk, as shown in Figure 3-9.

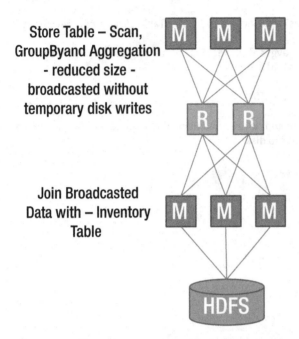

Store Table – Scan, GroupByand Aggregation - reduced size - broadcasted without temporary disk writes

Join Broadcasted Data with – Inventory Table

Figure 3-9. Hive query execution with the Tez engine

Pipelining the Data for Joins

Some SQL queries—especially in large data warehouses—involve star or snowflake schemas. The joins across the fact tables generally involve a lot of the data from the dimension tables too. These dimension tables are not generally small, especially if the dimensions have a lot of attributes. In such cases, broadcasting may not be an option, in terms of efficiency.

Under such conditions, Tez allows records from one data node to be streamed to the next. This allows Hive to build a pipeline of in-memory joins that can efficiently stream records during the join process.

Dynamically Partitioned Joins

In cases in which the tables to be joined are already partitioned or bucketed, and the table on the right side of the JOIN clause is *not* small enough to be broadcasted to all the Map or Reduce processes in the next layer, Tez just transmits the right partitions to the process in the next layers that are required by them, based on the partitioning/bucketing information. This works very well when the Hash join algorithm is used to perform joins.

For example, take the following SQL query (seen earlier, under "Optimization by Using a Broadcast Join"). Assume that both the tables are partitioned/bucketed on the join key, and the inventory table is not small enough to be broadcasted to all the processes.

```
SELECT sales.item, sales.quantity,inventory.quantityleft
FROM sales JOIN inventory
ON (sales.productId = inventory.productID)
```

In this case, Tez would optimize the SQL query by broadcasting to the later processes, not the whole table to the later processes in the chain, but only the correct partitions from the right-hand side of the table (see Figure 3-10).

Scan RHS Table - Inventory (smaller) and Broadcast Partitions

Join – Sales Partitions with Broadcasted Partitions of Inventory

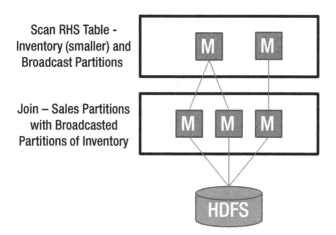

Figure 3-10. *Tez optimizations for JOIN query execution*

Vectorization of Queries

Vectorized query execution is a Hive feature that greatly reduces the CPU usage for queries such as table scans, filters, aggregates, and joins. Typically, a query processor will scan and process one row at a time. Processing rows one at a time results in poor CPU utilization and a larger number of CPU instructions. What vectorized query execution does is process a block of rows at a time. In other words, the idea is to process a batch of rows as an array of column vectors. Within each such block, a column of vectors of primitive types is stored, either in compressed or uncompressed form.

A one-row-at-a-time-based execution model is essentially very slow. There are a couple of primary reasons for this. Because Hive internally uses object inspectors, which enable a good level of abstraction, it has, however, a major cost implication. This cost implication gets worse because of lazy SerDe implementation within the internals of Hive. Each such loop for a row processing creates Java objects, which adds to the object creation overhead and time, and has a lot of if-then clauses and lots of CPU instructions. This also causes the CPU to stall, because it has to wait for the data to be fetched before it can start working.

However, operations on a block of data can be done quickly, by iterating through the block in a loop with very few branches, which is the core concept behind the speedup. These loops can then be compiled to very few streamlined operations, which can be completed in fewer CPU cycles, taking advantage of CPU cache and executing in fewer clock cycles. This makes an effective use of pipelining, which most modern CPU architectures are very effective at. Most of the primitive data types are supported as part of vectorized query execution.

Use of LLAP with Tez

One of the new additions to Hive is a new execution model that is a combination of process-based tasks and long-lived daemons running on worker nodes. LLAP (Long Live and Process) is a long-lived daemon process on the data nodes within the Hive framework that reduces the startup costs of tasks and gives the JIT (just in time) compiler a few extra ms with which to optimize the code. LLAP is an in-memory columnar cache that replaces direct interactions with the DataNode.

Functionality such as caching, pre-fetching, query fragment processing, and access control can be moved into the daemon. Small queries can be processed by the LLAP daemon directly, while any resource-intensive queries can be performed inside YARN containers.

LLAP is not an execution engine or a storage layer. The idea of introducing LLAP was to improve the latency of the queries with some local caching. The LLAP process has a number of executors within it, and each of them executes some task of the Map or Reduce process.

An LLAP process is an optional daemon process running on multiple nodes with the following capabilities:

- Caching and data reuse across queries with compressed columnar data in-memory (off-heap)

- Multi-threaded execution, including reads with predicate pushdown and hash joins

- High throughput I/O using Asynchronous Elevator algorithms with dedicated thread and core per disk

- Granular column level security across applications

This hybrid engine approach provides fast response times by efficient in-memory data caching and low-latency processing, provided by node-resident LLAP processes.

LLAP enables efficient execution of queries by approaches such as caching columnar data, building JIT-friendly operator pipelines, and adding new performance-enhancing features like asynchronous I/O, pre-fetching, and multi-threaded processing (see Figure 3-11).

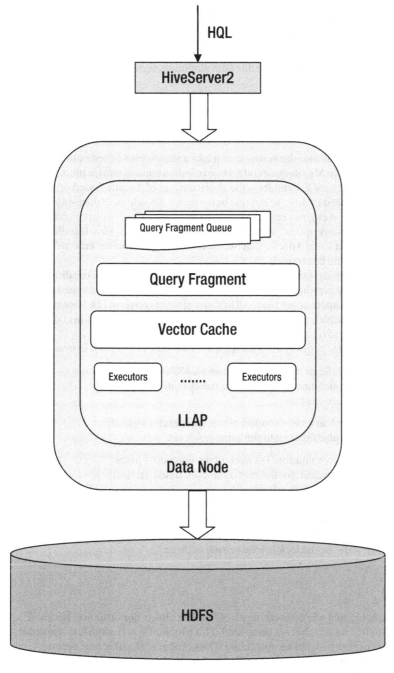

Figure 3-11. *LLAP architecture*

LLAP works only with the TEZ engine, does not currently support ACID-based transactions in Hive, and only supports the ORC format.

All these optimizations enable Hive to execute not only ETL/ELT workloads but also such applications as data discovery. The ability to work interactively with SQL on Hive expands the roles of Hive users and expedites development, testing, data flow, and data pipeline execution.

CBO Optimizers

When Hive originally came into the ecosystem, it had a simple rule-based optimizer to translate SQL queries into MapReduce code. Hive relied on some complex hints from the end user embedded in the SQL to address the shortcomings of the rule-based optimizer. These hints would be used to drive selections between a map-side vs. reduce-side join.

Relational databases engines reflect more than 30-plus years of research and development work in query optimization. Starting from version 0.13, Hive introduced cost-based optimization using Apache Calcite. Calcite is an open source, enterprise-grade CBO and query execution framework.

CBO generates efficient execution plans by examining the tables and conditions (filter, join) in the query to reduce latency and resource utilization. Calcite uses a plan pruner to select the cheapest query plan. All SQL queries are converted by Hive to a physical operator tree, which is then converted to MapReduce jobs. This conversion includes SQL parsing and transforming and operator-tree optimization.

Inside the CBO, an SQL query goes through the following four phases of evaluation:

1. Parse and validate query. It generates an AST (abstract syntax tree) for a valid query that contains the operations/operators the code must execute.

2. Generate exhaustive execution plans. It generates logically equivalent plans that yield the same result set.

3. Perform cost evaluation. For each of the preceding plans generated, it calculates the execution cost, based on heuristic statistics (cardinality, selectivity).

4. Choose the best low-cost plan.

Two of the biggest challenges for a query optimizer are how to leverage the join ordering and table sizes. Let us look briefly at each of them.

Join Order

The order of tables joined while executing an SQL query affects performance, because of the intermediate data sets that are generated. This problem is very similar to the order in which a series of matrices can be multiplied. The number of possible join orders increases exponentially with the number of tables involved, and it is not possible to evaluate the cost of execution of each such join order. The idea is to find the join order that results in the maximum reduction of intermediate rows generated, or, in other words, select the join order that is the most selective in terms of reducing or initially pruning the data sets. If the least amount of data sets that are to be worked on by later operators is identified early enough, this automatically speeds up the queries.

Join orders can be of three types: left-deep, bushy, and right-deep.

A left-deep join tree is shown in Figure 3-12.

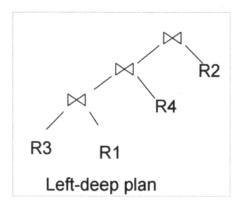

Figure 3-12. *Left-deep query plan*

A left-deep join tree does *not* produce efficient plans for snowflake schemas.

Bushy Trees

In the case of bushy trees, the join occurs on the results of two other joins, rather than on one table being scanned. It is very useful for snowflake schemas. These trees contain subtrees that can reduce the size of the intermediate data. The other advantage of a bushy tree is that the joins can be done in parallel, which could yield better performance, depending on the infrastructure and I/O patterns (see Figure 3-13).

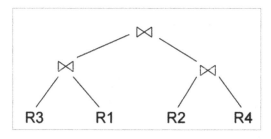

Figure 3-13. *Bushy query plan*

Table Sizing

CBO relies heavily on the statistics present in the Hive metastore for the table and columns to make the best query execution plans. These statistics include row counts, column distinct values, boundary statistics, and data distribution metrics. This helps the optimizer decide the type of algorithm to apply, based on whether the full table can be cached in-memory or the query processing requires swapping of the data to disk.

Recommendations to Speed Up Hive

In the last section of this chapter, we've outlined some of the very high-level approaches one can take to improve Hive performance. The following is by no means an exhaustive list, however.

Here are some recommendations to speed up Hive:

- Use the Tez or Spark engine and not MapReduce. Set the configuration to hive.execution.engine=tez or hive.execution.engine=spark, to use a different engine from the default MapReduce.

- Use Partitions and Bucketing wherever possible, if your data sets allow it and your data processing pipelines make it feasible. This drastically reduces the join time, because, in such cases, Hive only looks at a small fragment of the data sets when it does the join.

- Always enable statistics on Hive tables. This can help the CBO optimizer to build the best plan, based on actual data rather than plain heuristics.

- If you are on the latest version of Hive, make sure hive.vectorized.execution.enabled = true is turned on. Older versions of Hive had some problems with vectorization that are now resolved.

- Use ORC. Hive is optimized to work best with the ORC format, and, wherever possible, convert non-ORC tables to the ORC format before doing analytics or running SQL queries on the data. Using ORC and vectorization provides a lot of speedup with very little effort.

- When you have complex SQL queries that involve subqueries, make sure the subqueries are rewritten to temporary tables before the actual higher level query executes. It has been seen that this pattern always yields better performance than letting Hive work with subqueries directly.

Upcoming Features in Hive

Still missing from Hive are features such as referential integrity, unique constraints, secondary indexes, and other multiple types of indexes. Hive has had indexes for quite a while now, but their usage in real-life applications has been very minimal. There is no plan to support any of these features in the near future.

The latest version of Hive 2.0 has added the following capabilities from an SQL and performance perspective:

- Metastore support on HBase

- LLAP support

- Support for Hive Procedural Language, which implements procedural SQL for Hive

- Multiple features to support integration of Hive with Apache Spark

The following are some of the major still remaining functionalities to be supported by Hive:

- *Support for Theta join*: With this, tables can be joined on non-equality-based conditions on the columns.

- *Support for GeoSpatial analytics*

- *Support for updatable views*: Views have existed in Hive for a while, and all relational databases support updatable views with their own rules. Updatable views in Hive can help in some ETL-related tasks, especially when the underlying data changes.

Summary

This chapter covered Hive, from a high level as well as from a deep architectural perspective, detailing how a complex SQL on a Hadoop engine such as Hive is engineered, both from functionality and performance aspects.

In the next chapter, we will discuss some of the SQL engines for interactive and ad hoc query analysis, in which improving the latency of SQL queries is the main objective.

■ ■ ■

Interactive SQL— Architecture

In the last chapter, we discussed in depth the architectural details of Hive and the batch-processing-based SQL engine on Hadoop. We learned about its architecture, components, and features, and how it is evolving to keep pace with the technology innovations.

In this chapter, we will discuss the internal details of SQL on Hadoop engines for interactive workloads. The chapter primarily focuses on the architecture and internals of SQL engines that fall into the interactive category and their approaches to executing ad hoc SQL queries with low latency on large data sets.

Why Is Interactive SQL So Important?

Interactive querying of big data is primarily for supporting data discovery, data exploration, and speed of thought-based data analysis capabilities. Allowing interactive ad hoc queries is essential, as more often than not, the user does not necessarily know all the questions to ask of the data ahead of time. As questions are asked and answers obtained, it raises new questions, based on thought process, to the answers to previous queries. During this process of asking new questions based on results obtained from previous queries, it is important to provide low latency; otherwise, the train of thought for a given user could be lost.

In the new world of big data, business intelligence (BI) and visual analytics tools are evolving to interactively work with big data ecosystems. Interactive workloads include the ability to execute ad hoc SQL queries on the data, through either front-end tools, APIs, or the command line. These interactive workload-class SQL engines execute ad hoc queries using a variety of optimization techniques on large-scale data sets, to return the results in the shortest possible time.

Currently, for interactive analysis, the pattern is to apply ETL (Extract, Transform, Load) to data from different source systems, prepare the data so that it is compatible for fast data access, and build a new data set that has aggregated information for best latency and I/O load characteristics. In other words, ETL is initially used to prepare the data to expedite data loading, preparing new data sets containing aggregated information, to make it efficient for BI tools to provide faster response time for downstream ad hoc analytic queries. This pattern has been used in the past in typical data warehouses and

© Sumit Pal 2016
S. Pal, *SQL on Big Data*, DOI 10.1007/978-1-4842-2247-8_4

to build materialized views and data marts, but it inherently suffers from impedance mismatches and delays in the actual analysis, due to data preparation tasks.

At a high level, interactive SQL on Hadoop engines has the following challenges:

- *Low latency*: Response times for interactive queries should be significantly faster than with batch processes.

- *ANSI SQL compatibility*: Ensuring that interactive SQL engines on big data are used by the BI tools also presents the challenge of supporting the SQL ANSI standards and compatibility issues, to find broad applicability and usage.

- *High concurrency*: As these tools get better at providing low latency, more and more users adopt and use them, which gives rise to another challenge that these engines have to address: keeping low latency with high concurrency. It is an extremely challenging proposition to keep low-latency service-level agreements (SLAs) with high concurrency on large-scale data sets.

- *Federated data sources*: The ability to query data that is set across multiple different data sources, different formats, and different locations and form holistic results that select subsets of attributes from each of the data sets to get the answer.

Interactive SQL engines on big data is a fiercely competitive field in which both commercial and open source products are coming up with innovative ideas and architectures to address the challenges. This chapter will cover some of the popular SQL-on-big-data engines: Spark SQL, Impala, Apache Drill, Jethro, and Vertica.

SQL Engines for Interactive Workloads

In this section, we will look at quite a few SQL engines that fall into the category of interactive SQL engines for big data.

Spark

Apache Spark is an in-memory distributed computing platform for fast general-purpose data processing and computation. Spark supports different types of computations—batch, interactive, stream processing, and iterative machine-learning algorithms—on the same framework. One of the distinguishing features of Spark is its ability to run computations in memory and store intermediate results in memory without going to disk.

Because varying workloads can be supported within the same framework and processing engine, Spark is a very convenient and productive framework to use from code development, code maintenance, and deployment perspectives. This is so because developers, devops, and dataops teams have to learn only one framework—its internals, nuances, and best practices—rather than different frameworks for different workloads. This also has been the major reason for adoption of Spark as a distributed processing framework.

We will not go into detail about Spark, because this is not a Spark-related book, but we will cover how Spark SQL is engineered and architected for interactive SQL queries.

Spark Stack

Figure 4-1 shows the Spark component stack, in which the bottom layer is the cluster operating system (OS), such as Yarn, Mesos, or Standalone Spark. The cluster OS is meant to abstract out the details of the cluster related to resource management, scheduling, and fault tolerance from the higher layers.

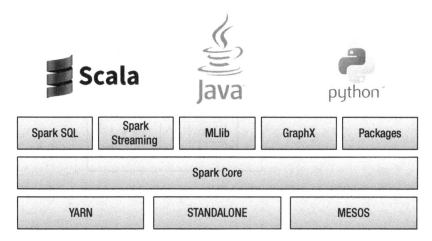

Figure 4-1. *Spark component stack*

Spark Core, which contains RDDs (Resilient Distributed Datasets), optimizers, and DAG (Directed Acyclic Graph), is built on top of the cluster OS, while the major components that developers use reside a layer above the core Spark framework—Spark SQL, Spark Streaming, MLlib, and GraphX for machine learning algorithms.

Spark Architecture

At a very high level, Figure 4-1 describes the Spark architecture stack, while Figure 4-2 shows how a Spark application works. A Spark application is composed of drivers, workers, executors, and tasks. The Spark driver starts the Spark worker processes on nodes in the cluster. Each Spark worker process spawns executors that spawn tasks, which are threads of the same code executing on different pieces of the data. The executor process coordinates the execution of the tasks and the details around them, such as scheduling, fault tolerance, etc., while the worker process communicates with the driver process.

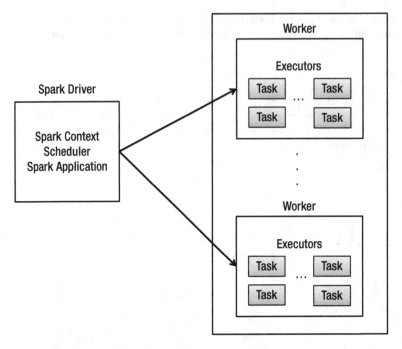

Figure 4-2. *Spark deployment architecture*

Spark SQL

Spark SQL supports interacting with the Spark engine using SQL and HiveQL. Spark SQL represents structured data, as Spark DataFrames, which are internally represented as Spark RDDs with an associated schema. Spark SQL allows developers to mix SQL queries with code written with any of the language bindings supported in Spark—Python, Java, Scala, and R—all within a single application. The whole idea of providing an SQL layer on top of the Spark engine framework is to support the following:

- Writing less code

- Reading less code

- Allowing the Spark Catalyst optimizer (discussed later in this chapter) to do most of the hard work of figuring out where, when, and how to execute the query, so that it is best optimized, has low latency, and does the least amount of work to obtain the results.

The Spark SQL library is composed of the following components:

- *Data Source API*: This is an API for loading/saving data from any data source.

- *DataFrame API*: This is the API for higher level representation for data, used directly by the application developers.

- *SQL optimizer*: This is a rule-based optimizer to optimize the data transformations specified in SQL.

Data Source API is a universal API for loading/saving data, with support for data sources such as Hive and NoSQL databases, flat files, and data formats such as Avro, JSON, JDBC, and Parquet. It allows third-party integration through Spark packages. For example, the built-in comma-separated value (CSV) data source API allows for

- Loading/Saving CSV data

- Automatic schema discovery within the CSV file

- Automatic data type inference

The Data Source API can also automatically prune columns and push filters to the source, as the first steps to optimize the data access.

The DataFrame is a distributed collection of rows organized into named columns. DataFrame is a data structure for structured data, whereas RDD is a data structure for unstructured data. DataFrame, in other words, is the combination of RDD plus schema. The DataFrame API in Spark is inspired from R data frames and Python panda libraries, which support data processing and data wrangling of structured data.

A Data Source API implementation returns DataFrames, which provide the ability to combine data from multiple sources and provide uniform access from different language APIs. Having a single data structure allows users to build multiple DSLs (Domain Specific Languages) targeting different developers, but all such DSLs eventually use the same optimizer and code generator. A high-level Spark SQL architecture and how the Data Source API and DataFrame API interact is shown in Figure 4-3.

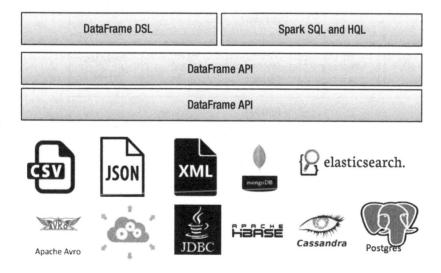

Figure 4-3. *Spark SQL components and architecture*

Spark SQL Architecture

As shown in Figure 4-4 and Figure 4-5, the elegance of DataFrame design is that it allows a uniform abstraction layer on top of the core Spark libraries for different data processing tasks. This allows a developer to do data frame-based development work for SQL as well as for streaming applications or data processing on GraphX or GraphFrames (introduced in Spark 1.6).

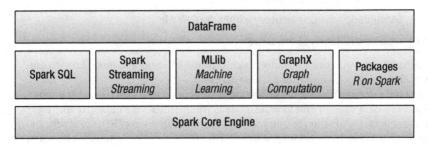

Figure 4-4. *DataFrame and Spark components*

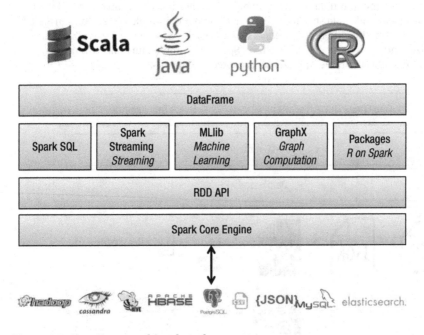

Figure 4-5. *DataFrame and Spark stack*

Figure 4-6 shows how DataFrame and the Catalyst optimizer are the major underlying underpinnings of the whole SQL-on-Spark stack architecture. Any SQL query—HQL, SQL, or queries originating from a DSL-based Spark application—is processed by the Spark SQL engine and goes through the DataFrame library and Catalyst optimizer layer. This provides the same kind of optimization for any of these queries, irrespective of their point of origin.

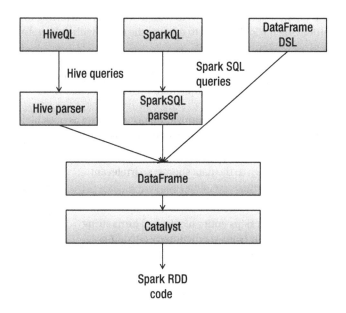

Figure 4-6. *Spark SQL pipeline*

With the introduction of the DataFrame abstraction, multiple DSLs can now share the same optimizer and execution engines, and all DSLs generate code based on the DataFrame API.

Spark SQL Optimization—Catalyst Optimizer

Catalyst is a query plan optimizer. It is a rule-based framework that

- allows developers to plug custom rules specific to their DSL for adding new forms of optimizations to query execution; and

- allows extensibility of existing rules to add data-source-specific rules that can push filtering or aggregation into external storage systems or to support new data types.

The Catalyst optimizer is based on functional programming constructs available in the Scala language. It supports both rule-based and cost-based optimization.

One of the first steps for executing an SQL query is transformation of the query into a DataFrame API, which is also a logical plan representation of the query. The logical plan is the tree representation of the query. Every transformation in Spark is essentially modeled as a tree, which is optimized by the Catalyst optimizer's built-in rules. The logical plan goes through a series of rules to resolve and optimize the execution plan, and after optimization, the logical plan is converted to a physical plan for actual execution of the query.

Spark SQL, along with the Catalyst optimizer, helps to read less data by converting to more efficient formats and modifying the logical plan to execute the query with the lowest possible latency.

Catalyst optimizes the logical plan by rearranging the query operators and lower-level operations. As an example, the Catalyst optimizer might decide to move a filter operation before a join operation—a very typical example to reduce the data that is operated on during the join execution phase.

Because Spark is a lazy execution framework, optimization occurs as late as possible; therefore, Spark SQL can optimize across functions. Some of the optimizations that Catalyst performs include the following:

- It pushes filter predicates down to the data source, so irrelevant data can be skipped right at the source, thus reducing unnecessary data movement.

- When reading Parquet files, it skips entire blocks and turns string comparisons to integer comparisons via dictionary encoding, which results in faster operations.

- Catalyst compiles operations into physical plans and generates highly optimized Java virtual machine (JVM) bytecodes.

- It intelligently chooses between broadcast joins and shuffle joins, to reduce network traffic.

- It eliminates expensive object allocations and reduces virtual function calls.

When the DataFrame is cached in memory by the Spark code, the Catalyst optimizer automatically calculates the statistics—maximum and minimum values of a column, number of distinct and NULL values—which it later uses to skip some partitions while running filter-based SQL queries, resulting in additional performance improvements.

The Catalyst optimizer is also a compiled library to manipulate trees, in this case, a logical plan tree specific to relational query processing, to move around nodes, remove edges, and short-circuit branches. Internally, it applies pattern matching recursively across the tree, to apply the optimization rules and update the tree with the best execution plan.

In Figure 4-7, you will see the different steps through which an SQL query has to go through in order to be ready for execution. These sets of steps are generally the same across most of the SQL engines. The core difference between SQL engines is in the middle sections, where the optimizer steps in to build the best optimized plan, based on different criteria. These optimization criteria could be based on rules, code generation, and query-execution costs. The core IP of SQL engines lies in this optimizer layer, to lower the SQL data-processing latencies.

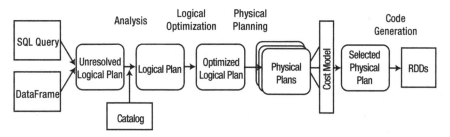

Figure 4-7. *Catalyst optimizer role in query processing*

The final piece of work that the Catalyst optimizer does is code generation. For workloads that are CPU-bound, any optimization at the code-execution level for each row of data to be processed can result in massive speedups for large data sets. Imagine if you can shave off 1 microsecond of query execution time from a single row of data, for big data sets having a billion row data, the query engine would be 1000 seconds faster. This is the extreme to which the Catalyst optimizer works to improve the query speed.

Code generation is an extensive and complex topic in itself, and we will not go into too much detail about it here. Essentially, the Catalyst optimizer uses a special feature of the Scala language called quasiquotes that allows automatic generation of abstract syntax trees (AST), which are fed to the Scala compiler to generate bytecodes.

An expression used in the SQL query is converted to AST by Catalyst, which is then worked upon by Scala code to evaluate the expression and then compile and run the generated code. Without code generation, simple expressions within an SQL query, such as (Col1 + Col2)*2, would have to be parsed and interpreted for each row of data. This could result in lots of overhead, especially CPU branching and virtual function calls, which can slow down processing.

Spark SQL with Tachyon (Alluxio)

Tachyon, now called Alluxio, is an in-memory file system that enables reliable data sharing across data-processing frameworks such as Spark and MapReduce. Tachyon achieves high performance by using memory caching and internally using lineage information. It caches a working set of files in memory and avoids going to disk.

Tachyon with Spark SQL has been used successfully at Baidu to provide low-latency ad hoc SQL query to data warehouses for business analysts. The addition of Tachyon to Spark SQL provides 10–20 times the speed for analytic query processing.

The initial computes are done in Spark engine, but the results are then cached within the Tachyon file system. Within Spark, SQL calls can be made using the DataFrame to the data stored on Tachyon.

After the query parsing and optimization is done within the Spark SQL engine, the query executor checks whether the requested data is already cached within the Tachyon file system. If so, it reads from Tachyon; otherwise, a new Spark job is initiated to read from the data store the computations done within the Spark engine, which are then cached in the Tachyon file system.

Analytic Query Support in Spark SQL

Spark started supporting analytic functions from version 1.4. Addition of windowing functions to Spark improves the expressiveness of DataFrame and Spark SQL. Spark supports three basic kinds of analytic functions: ranking (rank, dense_rank, ntile, row_number), analytic (first_value, last_value, lead, lag), and aggregate.

With Spark SQL, the window functions are used with the OVER clause.

When using the DataFrame API, one uses the function name followed by the OVER clause.

Inside the OVER clause is the window specification, which consists of the partitioning (which decides what rows are to be part of the same partition as the given row in question), Order (how the rows inside a partition are ordered), and Frame (the rows to be included, based on the current row in question) specification.

In SQL parlance, it would look something like OVER (PARTITION BY ... ORDER BY ... frame_type BETWEEN start AND end).

While in the DataFrame API world it would look like the following:

```
windowSpec = Window.partitionBy(...).orderBy(...)
windowSpec.rowsBetween(start, end)
```

The frame specification is more detailed, with lots of options, and the frame_type can be either – ROW/RANGE.

Start can be either UNBOUNDEDPRECEDING, CURRENT ROW, <value> PRECEDING, and <value> FOLLOWING; and end can be either UNBOUNDED, FOLLOWING, CURRENT ROW, <value> PRECEDING, and <value> FOLLOWING.

Spark 2.0 introduced built-in support for time windows. These behave very similarly to the Spark streaming time windows.

General Architecture Pattern

In the next few sections, we take a deeper look at some of the state-of-the-art massive parallel processing (MPP) analytic processing engines for big data processing. Impala from Cloudera (now open source) and Apache Drill are the two MPP SQL engines we will cover in the following sections. The core ideas for these two MPP engines have evolved from Google's Dremel, which introduced two main innovations: handling nested data with column-striped formats and multilevel query execution trees, which allow parallel processing of large data sets over large-scale computing clusters. Both these MPP engines rely on full scan to return the relevant data but also on smart optimizations to figure out what to scan before the actual scanning process starts.

Impala

One of the initial main goals of Impala was to provide an SQL-on-Hadoop solution for fast interactive workloads. Impala is part of the crowded marketplace of low-latency SQL engines on large data sets for analytic queries.

Like all MPP SQL engines, Impala is architected to be a shared nothing architecture in which all the processors are loosely coupled, have their own memory and CPU, and own chunks of data to work with. Impala is designed for analytic workloads, rather than transaction or operational workloads.

However, unlike other high-cost MPP engines out there, Impala has been designed to scale out by adding commodity servers to the Impala cluster. Impala has been designed to work as the back-end engine of BI tools for fast analytic queries on large data sets, and it supports application connectivity with support for Java Database Connectivity (JDBC) and open database connectivity (ODBC).

Impala has been written in the C++ language to increase its speed and make possible lots of machine-generated code for faster execution. As an engine based on C++, Impala avoids many of the problems associated with Java-based engines related to garbage collection slowdowns and heap size issues. Impala is *not* a storage engine; it is an SQL query engine that leverages data stored on HDFS/HBase or flat files and directories. Impala uses an internal in-memory tuple format that puts fixed-width data at fixed offsets for faster data access. It uses special CPU instructions for text parsing and crc32 computation.

Impala Architecture

Impala uses its unique distributed query engine to minimize response time. This distributed query engine is installed on all data nodes in the cluster.

There were twofold architectural tenets for Impala. One was to make Impala extremely fast, to support the low-latency query requirement for SQL on large data sets. The other was to ensure its linear scalability. Impala optimizes CPU usage to get the query result in the shortest possible time. Impala recommends using servers with large memory, preferably 96GB+, in addition to servers with modern chipsets, such as Sandybridge. Impala heavily leverages modern CPU instructions for fast code generation and speeding up queries on large data sets.

In this section, we discuss the main components that make Impala a low-latency SQL query engine. Let us start by looking at Figure 4-8.

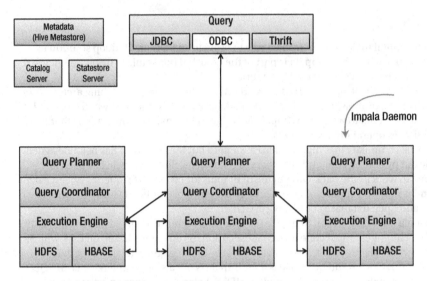

Figure 4-8. Impala architecture and the components

Impala comprises three main daemons (long-running processes) that handle the functionalities that Impala needs to process a query. Impala daemons are installed in each of the data nodes. This is done during the installation phase of Impala. Impala daemons run on the same node from where the data is to be queried, preserving the data locality. Each Impala daemon is an isolated process in the shared nothing architecture.

The Impala node to which the clients (e.g., impala-shell) are connected plays the role of query planner/coordinator, while the other nodes are the query execution engines. In other words, one Impala daemon acts as a leader, while the other Impala daemons running on each Hadoop data node act as execution engines. Outlined following are the main components of the Impala engine.

> *impalad*: The brain behind Impala is the query engine. Its function is to process queries using all the optimization rules built within the engine, to access and process the data in the most efficient manner. Impala relies heavily on the data distribution and block placement capabilities of HDFS, to ensure data locality for each impalad. The impalad process has three components: the Query Planner, the Query Coordinator, and the Query Executor. The Query Planner syntactically and semantically validates the query, transforms it to a logical and physical plan, and, finally, compiles the plan into a physical distributed query plan made up of query fragments, which are taken by the Query Coordinators to execute. impalad processes data blocks in the data node where it is executing and reads the data directly from the local disk. This minimizes network load and benefits from the file cache on the data nodes.

statestored: This maintains the status of the other Impala daemons running on the data nodes, where status includes information about the health of the node. This daemon monitors the health of impalad on all the nodes in a cluster. If by chance an impalad daemon becomes unresponsive, the statestore daemon communicates with other nodes in the cluster, and subsequent queries do not involve the unresponsive impala node. This daemon has only one running process.

catalog server: This daemon synchronizes the metadata of the tables with impalad, guaranteeing that all of impalad's metadata is in sync. There is only one instance of this daemon running in the cluster.

Queries can be submitted to Impala through either Impala Shell or JDBC/ODBC drivers. Once a query is submitted, the query planner process turns the query request into a collection of plan fragments, and then the coordinator initiates execution on a remote impalad. Intermediate results are streamed between impalad's before the query results are streamed back to client.

The coordinator orchestrates interactions between impalad across all the data nodes and also aggregates results produced by each data node. impalad also exposes a remote procedure call (RPC) interface that other impalad can use to connect to exchange data. Also, this interface allows the coordinator to assign work for each impalad.

Following query submission by the client, the usual steps of query validation, syntax and semantic analysis, are done before the query is optimized by the query engine. Every query is first validated syntactically and semantically, to make sure that there are no errors in the user's query, both from a syntax perspective as well as from a semantic perspective, ensuring that the query makes sense. The metadata for the query exists in the Hive metastore. After this step, query planning occurs, whereby Impala tries to figure out the best way to solve the query to get the results. The EXPLAIN query dumps the output of what is going on within Impala to figure out the way to solve the problem. The EXPLAIN query provides an outline of the steps that impalad will perform and the relevant details on how the workload will be distributed among the nodes.

Optimization involves generating the best physical plan for the query, in terms of cost of execution as well as code generation of the query for faster execution on the hardware. The optimized query is submitted to the coordinator process, which orchestrates the query execution. When a query executes, the coordinator orchestrates interactions between Impala nodes, and once the result is available from each impalad process, it aggregates the results. This coordinator process is part of the impalad process and resides in all the nodes. Any node can act as the query coordinator. It is the coordinator that assigns work units to the impalad processes.

Once the work is assigned to each impalad process by the coordinator, the impalad process works with the storage engine to implement the query operators, for example, constant folding, predicate pushdown, etc., so as to extract only the relevant portions of the data that are really needed to satisfy the query.

The execution engine (executor process) in the impalad daemon executes the optimized query by reading from the data source at high speeds. It leverages all the disks and their controllers to read at an optimized speed and executes query fragments that have been optimized by the code optimizer, which includes Impala LLVM and the code-generation process. Impala executor serves hundreds of plan fragments at any given time.

Impala does nothing special for failover. Because HDFS provides failover using replication, if the impalad daemon is installed on the replicated nodes, the Impala process will seamlessly start using the impalad on the replicated nodes.

Impala Optimizations

Impala is built to take full advantage of modern-day hardware chips and the latest techniques for efficient query execution. Impala uses many tools and techniques to get the best query performance. Some of the techniques Impala uses for best performance are discussed following.

HDFS Caching

Impala can leverage HDFS (Hadoop distributed file system) caching to use the memory effectively, especially for repeated queries that take advantage of data pinned in memory, regardless of the size of the data being processed. With HDFS caching, one can designate a subset of frequently used data to be pinned in memory. This applies to tables or table partitions frequently accessed and small enough to fit in the HDFS memory cache.

Once HDFS caching is set up, within Impala DDL, CREATE and ALTER statements specify the cache pool name, to enable HDFS caching for that table. The actual syntax looks like CREATE TABLE ... CACHED IN <pool name> or ALTER TABLE ... SET CACHED IN <pool name>.

For a table that is already cached, if new partitions are added through ALTER TABLE ... ADD PARTITION statements, the data in those new partitions is automatically cached in the same pool.

File Format Selection

Different file formats and compression codecs work better for different data sets. Impala provides performance gains irrespective of file format; however, choosing the most optimized and efficient format for the data you work with yields further performance improvements. Better data formats allow users to leverage lower storage and optimization at query time, by processing less data, and also during I/O and network, by reading and transmitting less data.

Text format data is not efficient for storage and query, unlike Parquet and ORC, which are highly optimized file formats that result in better storage and I/O efficiency. Hence, is it always advisable to convert text data to a Parquet format, for which Impala is most optimized. If the data is available as a text file, create a new table with a Parquet format and use Impala to query that data format. Natively, Impala has been designed to work best with a Parquet format. Parquet has lots of optimizations built in, which makes it suitable for querying large data sets with low latency.

Optimizations in Parquet make it suitable for low-latency queries, which include those optimized for large data blocks and nested data. Internally, Parquet uses an extensible set of column encodings and also includes embedded inlined column statistics for optimization of scan efficiency through min/max values for a block.

Recommendations to Make Impala Queries Faster

Some of the recommended best practices and empirical rules to keep in mind to make queries run faster include the following:

- Use numeric types (not strings) when possible, because using string data types can result in higher memory consumption, more storage, and slower processing.

- Opt for a decimal data type rather than a float/double type.

- Identify query access patterns from the different use cases and create the right partitioning strategy, for example.

- Table columns used in WHERE clauses are possible choices for partition keys.

- Dates or spatial boundaries or geography can be good choices for partition keys.

- Make sure partition size is less than 100K or so.

- If possible, limit the columns to less than 2K. This can affect performance of the Hive metastore.

- Configure Impala to use Parquet and Snappy for best performance. If you've given any updates, opt for using Avro, for best performance.

- There is a fine line between block size selection. Larger blocks result in better throughput but lower parallelism, while the opposite is true for smaller block sizes.

- You should tune your memory requirements after gathering some query statistics, using the explain query plan feature. Look at the peak memory usage profile to get better estimates.

- Favor machines with 128GB of RAM and 10GB network interconnect.

- Use such tools as EXPLAIN, SUMMARY, and PROFILE, which return plan fragments without executing the query. SUMMARY gives an overview of the runtime statistics, and PROFILE gives an exhaustive listing of runtime statistics after query execution, for example, the number of rows processed and amount of memory consumed to run the query.

Code Generation

Impala extensively uses code generation to optimize CPU utilization and reduce latency, by utilizing the latest trends in modern CPUs. It is recommended that you run Impala on newer systems with more disks, because Impala can utilize the full bandwidth of available disks to improve I/O throughput. It is also recommended that you have nodes with large memory, because Impala benefits from being able to work with data in memory, which often results in lower latency of the SQL queries.

Code generation can dramatically improve CPU efficiency and query execution time. Query execution engines typically incur a lot of overhead in the following:

> *Virtual function calls*: Any expression in the SQL query incurs the overhead of being evaluated again and again for each row of data the engine processes. Even if the expression by itself is simple to evaluate, the underlying implementation causes virtual function calls to evaluate the expressions. This causes a huge CPU overhead of context switching, saving the current space in the stack, and calling the virtual function. Elimination of this overhead can shave off valuable time from the query execution perspective, if the virtual calls are inlined with code generation.

> *Switch statements*: Branching-based queries and branch instructions prevent effective instruction pipelining and instruction-level parallelism, and this can cause CPU inefficiency. The branch predictor can help in these circumstances, but code generation results in better speedups.

> *Propagating constant literals*: Any constant value used in the query can result in memory lookups by the engine when it is executing the query. This can add more latency and can be eliminated if the engine can fold these constants within the generated code.

> *LLVM*: Low Level Virtual Machine is an innovation that is applied by Impala to speed up queries and remove the previously mentioned overheads. You can think of LLVM as the JVM byte code generator. LLVM generates optimized code for the program you have written, using certain compiler flags. These kinds of optimum code generation are routinely done for code written in C/C++, based on the hardware platform in which they are deployed. The only difference, in this case, is that LLVM is generating optimized code for the SQL query to be executed. LLVM includes a set of libraries that are the building blocks of a compiler that is used to generate the code from the SQL query syntax tree. LLVM provides an API for code generation.

Post-SQL Semantic Analysis: The LLVM steps in and generates the code for the query operators, in which the SQL engine spends most of the CPU cycles. At this time, all the data types and the file formats are known, and application of the LLVM code generation technique here provides all the necessary function call inline generation to provide the maximum speedup.

By leveraging LLVM and code generation, Impala can speed up queries by three to five times. Code generation is applied to inner loops that are executed millions of times, especially in large data sets, and, if they shave off even a couple of microseconds from each row of a million row table, this results in multisecond speedups for a given query.

Figure 4-9 shows how Impala is leveraged by BI and Data Analysis tools to provide low-latency interactive queries. Impala provides ODBC drivers for external applications to connect and run SQL queries. During deployment, Impala needs the daemons to be installed on the data nodes. For certain deployments, this can be an issue, in terms of installations, maintenance, and upgrades.

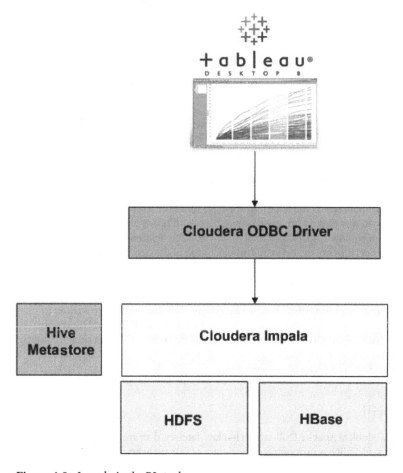

Figure 4-9. *Impala in the BI stack*

Impala processes reside on the same data nodes where the other processes reside and where ETL takes place. In order to have guaranteed SLAs, and for best Impala performance, it is always advisable to isolate the clusters for ETL workloads from the clusters for interactive workloads. In order to preserve data locality, this can necessitate data movement from the ETL clusters to interactive clusters.

SQL Enhancements and Impala Shortcomings

Let us look into why Impala and Hive show different performance characteristics in the response time to the same data. According to Cloudera, the following are the two main reasons for Impala's good performance:

1. Impala reduces CPU load by multiple optimization, as LLVM and by working on special chipsets, as compared to Hive, and, hence, can increase its I/O bandwidth, which is why it has better performance than Hive for pure I/O-bound workloads.

2. For long and complex queries, Hive has a multistage MR pipeline that results in multiple stages of reads and writes to disks, resulting in slowdowns. Impala avoids this by having a totally different engine that does not rely on MR but pipelines the data between the nodes, resulting in efficient usage of the intra-cluster network bandwidth.

Impala version 2.3 has built-in support for querying complex types in Parquet format: ARRAY, MAP, and STRUCTs. SQL queries can work directly on the nested data sets without the need to flatten the data before querying. Impala supports queries on complex data types, using join syntax rather than explode(), as in Hive.

Though the latest version of Impala has very good coverage of SQL queries in terms of its compatibility to SQL-2003 standards, Impala does still lag behind Hive in support of SQL support. Impala needs the Hive metastore to function. This can be a problem for certain deployments that do not need or use Hive. Most HiveQL SELECT and INSERT statements run unmodified with Impala. Hive functionality related to TRANSFORM, JSON, XML, and SerDe is not available in Impala. Some of the aggregate functions in Hive, such as covar* and percentile* are named differently in Impala.

Impala and Hive share the same metastore database, and their tables are often used interchangeably. Impala's SQL syntax follows the SQL-92 standard and includes many industry extensions in areas such as built-in functions. UDFs in Impala are written in C++, which makes them even faster. Impala does support scalar UDFs and UDAFs but currently does not support UDTFs (table functions). Impala only supports single-column distinct count queries. Impala can query data residing in HDFS or HBase. Impala's support for querying from JSON files is very new.

Apache Drill

In this section, we look at Apache Drill, which is a low-latency, distributed SQL engine for large-scale data sets. Drill has propounded the theory of SQL on everything (Figure 4-10), which illustrates the power of Apache Drill in its ability to query almost any data, irrespective of what format it is in and where it resides, using SQL. Drill has shown how to do SQL on any data source, whether that be RDBMS, NoSQL database, files of any format—structured, unstructured, or semi-structured—and even on directories that can contain files in multiple formats. This is shown in Figure 4-10.

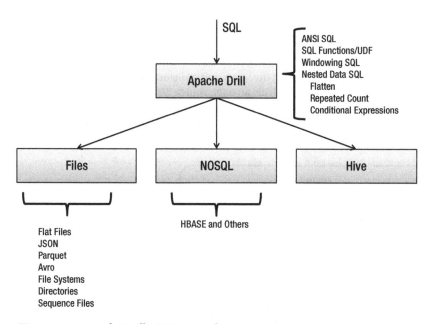

Figure 4-10. *Apache Drill—SQL everywhere*

Drill has been designed to scale out to thousands of nodes and query multi-terabytes of data at interactive speeds, which is very essential for BI and analytic tools. Drill supports SQL against a plethora of data sources—both relational, file-based data sources and NoSQL databases—as well as access to both structured and semi-structured data. Apache Drill is based partly on Google's research into building Dremel, which added innovations to generically handle nested data sets with columnar representation.

As with Impala, Apache Drill is not a storage engine—it is a query engine that can leverage a distributed framework architecture to scale out SQL queries across a cluster of machines on large data sets. Apache Drill relies completely on its modular and scalable architecture to perform low-latency SQL queries on multi-TB data sets. It does not rely on keeping any special indices or metadata for speeding up the queries and, like Impala, relies on building optimized full-table scans to get results.

Apache Drill Architecture

Apache Drill has a layered architecture, which comprises a user layer, processing layer, and data source layer. Apache Drill is a masterless architecture, with which a client can send a query to any node that works with other nodes in the cluster to execute the query and return the results.

The core of Apache Drill architecture is the drillbit, a process that is installed on all of the data nodes in the cluster. A drillbit can also be categorized as a service that takes queries from the client, processes the queries, and returns results.

A query can go to any of the drillbits. This becomes the initiator drillbit for that query. The initiator drillbit obtains the list of other available drillbit nodes in the cluster, while the client uses ZooKeeper to find any drillbit to which it can submit a query. The initiator drillbit determines the appropriate nodes in which queries can be executed, based on the data locality criteria for the best query execution.

Figure 4-11 shows the two major functionalities of a drillbit process: parsing and validating the syntax and semantics of the query and transforming the query to a logical plan. Internally, Drill uses Apache Calcite, an open source SQL parser, to parse queries. Drill's parser supports full ANSI SQL: 2003 standards and supports correlated subqueries, analytics functions, and ANSI SQL extensions for hierarchical data, which includes support for XML, JSON, BSON, and Avro and Protocol buffers.

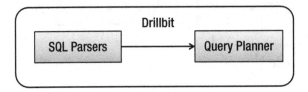

Figure 4-11. *Apache Drill—drillbits*

Internally, the logical plan can be either a set of objects within the system representing the query or a textual representation in the form of a JSON file. The logical plan describes the dataflow, using a data structure called a directed acyclic graph, which consists of a sequence of operators or nodes in the graph that describe the operations needed to arrive at the results.

This logical query is then optimized by the optimizer to a physical plan, which contains physical operators that are a description to the execution engine of how to execute the query. While optimizing the query, the optimizer takes into consideration the data formats of the data that is being queried, as well as the cluster sizing, etc., to prepare the optimized query plan. Drill uses standard database optimizations, both rule-based and cost-based, to rewrite and split the query. This is shown in Figure 4-12.

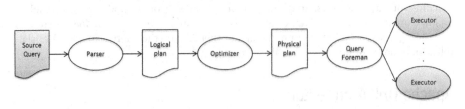

Figure 4-12. *Apache Drill—query processing and execution*

Once the optimized query plan is ready, it is processed by the executors. Query execution is distributed across multiple data nodes to address data locality. Results of queries are then aggregated locally, and aggregated results are transmitted to the executor that originated the query, as shown in Figure 4-13.

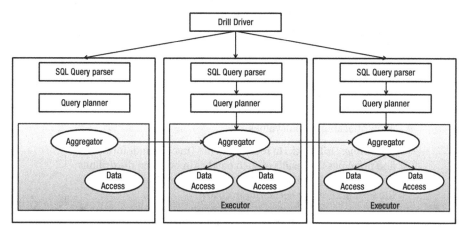

Figure 4-13. *Apache Drill—internal architecture*

Key Features

One of the beauties of Apache Drill's design and architecture is its extensibility. The logical plan can also be directly ingested into the system, if it is written as a DSL.

Apache Drill is designed from the ground up with well-designed APIs, having extensibility in mind . It supports the ability to write UDFs and allows a pluggable query language and the ability to write custom low-level operators. Apart from these, it also allows users to plug in new optimizers and to define scanners for new data sources and file formats.

One of the most highlighted features of Drill is its ability to read data sets with no schema defined up front, unlike Impala and Hive, in which schema definition is required before any query can be performed. Drill supports queries against unknown schemas, while the user has the flexibility to define a schema up front or allow Apache Drill to discover it. This almost achieves the holy grail of data warehousing, whereby you can avoid the whole ETL process of processing the data according to the schema before the data is used for analytics, reporting, or dashboards.

In short, the following is how Apache Drill is different when it comes to schemas:

- Apache Drill—schema discovery on the fly

- Relational Engines—schema on write

- Hive, Impala—schema on read

Drill has decentralized metadata, unlike Impala, so that it is not tied to a single Hive metastore for its metadata requirements. Queries can span tables from multiple Hive repositories, and the same query can refer to data sources from HBase or a distributed file store.

81

Query Execution

Drill is an MPP-based SQL query execution engine that performs distributed query processing across the nodes in the cluster.

During query execution, Drill optimizes for columnar storage and execution by using an in-memory columnar data model. With columnar data formats, Drill avoids disk access for columns not used in the query. Drill's execution layer performs SQL processing directly on columnar data, without any intermediate conversion to row-oriented data. Drill's query engine is characterized by

- *Columnar/Vectorized*: Drill operates on more than one record at a time with SIMD-based optimized instructions using LLVM and JVM optimizations. Internally Drill also maintains bitmaps to allow checking for null values.

- *Pipelining*: Drill works in record batches (in columnar format) and pipelines the results of such batches in between the drillbits on each node. Pipelining occurs in memory and, hence, reduces the serialization/de-serialization costs.

Drill's query engine is characterized by the following:

- Runtime compilation

- Late binding

- Extensibility

Figure 4-14 show the sequence of steps in Apache Drill for an SQL query execution as it occurs across the different layers of the product.

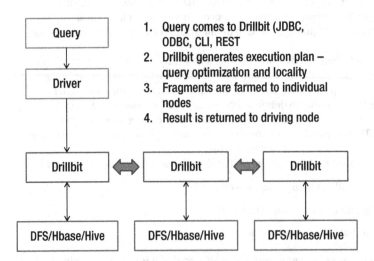

Figure 4-14. Apache Drill—query execution process

Apache Drill is a very mature product—more mature than Impala or Apache Spark. Selecting the right SQL-on-big-data engine depends to a certain extent on the kind of Hadoop distribution your organizations has. If it has Cloudera as the Hadoop distribution, Impala is probably the best way to go. If it has MapR distribution, definitely use Apache Drill. If you are using Apache Spark as your framework for different workloads, it is worth giving Spark SQL a try for your interactive queries to see how it performs.

Spark SQL is very new and evolving in terms of its support for SQL coverage and analytic queries.

If you are starting from a blank slate, it is recommended that you use Apache Drill before trying other products on the market. Apache Drill is a very versatile product, reflecting the kind of talent behind it. Apache Drill has wide support for a variety of data types, data sources, and complex SQL queries.

Vertica

One of the first commercial implementations of columnar databases was Vertica. It was largely based on C-Store and MonetDB. Vertica is optimized for large-scale analytics designed with a distributed compressed columnar architecture, which makes it faster for modern analytics workloads. It is an MPP platform that uses commodity servers and distributes its workload using a shared-nothing architecture. It is both a query and a storage engine. The query engine is highly optimized for querying the data in the fastest possible way.

Vertica is architected to reduce latency by lowering I/O, reading only necessary data using a highly compressed columnar format. It provides high scalability, with no single point of failure. Vertica SQL is fully ANSI SQL 99 compliant.

Vertica with Hadoop

Hadoop is best-suited for tasks involving large-scale ETL workloads on structured and unstructured data sets. Vertica works best on structured data, for low-latency complex analytic SQL queries. With Vertica's connectors to Hadoop and other big data tools, analysts can use familiar BI/analytics tools that generate SQL code to interact with any Hadoop distribution using Vertica.

The major use cases of Hadoop and Vertica are in conjunction with the following:

Use Hadoop to do ETL and then push the results required by BI tools and dashboards to Vertica for data analytics. These tools can query data seamlessly through Vertica, using Vertica's SQL interface, irrespective of whether the data resides in an optimized Vertica store or on HDFS as external Vertica tables. Both are accessed using SQL queries.

Vertica can query data from its native data store or from Hadoop, using connectors. The Vertica connector for Hadoop allows these two platforms to take advantage of their strengths. With the Vertica Hadoop connector, one can use data from Vertica in a Hadoop job and store the results of a Hadoop job in a Vertica database. Vertica can directly read data stored in HDFS in such formats as ORC, Parquet, and Avro.

Vertica is installed in its own cluster (see Figure 4-15 and Figure 4-16), which is separate from the Hadoop cluster. However, Vertica can be co-located within the same nodes as your Hadoop cluster. This deployment option should be selected with care, because most Hadoop installations are used primarily for ETL and data storage, while Vertica is used for low-latency analytical queries. If the Vertica engine is co-located with the Hadoop data nodes, guaranteeing SLAs for Vertica can be difficult, because it is hard to predict load on Hadoop nodes. This can be adjusted using the right capacity scheduling options with YARN on Hadoop, though nodes with Vertica installed may not be able to leverage YARN, because HP Vertica for SQL on Hadoop does not currently support the YARN resource manager.

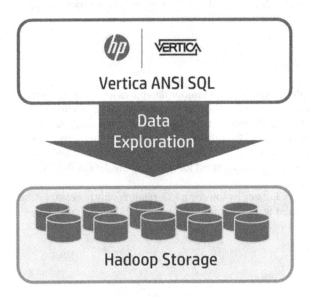

Figure 4-15. *Vertica integration with HDFS*

Vertica integrates with Hadoop using Vertica's in-house developed Hadoop connector, which is an implementation of the input and output APIs of Hadoop (see Figure 4-16). In this book, we will not go into the details or architecture of these APIs.

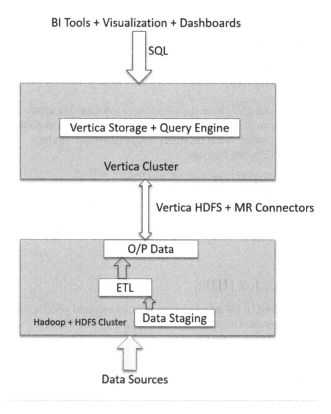

Figure 4-16. *Vertica accessing data in HDFS through connectors*

Vertica's HDFS connector is used to create and query external tables, reading the data in place, i.e., from HDFS, and not making additional copies into Vertica's own format. The HDFS connector can be used with any data format for which a parser is available. The connector is installed and runs on each node in the Hadoop cluster.

There are actually two Vertica to Hadoop connectors.

Hadoop MapReduce Connector

This is used to create Hadoop MapReduce jobs that read and write data to HP Vertica. This connector is used in the following instances:

- When a MapReduce job requires data stored in Vertica

- When MapReduce jobs directly inserts data into Vertica for analysis in real time, using Vertica's out-of-the-box SQL capabilities for advanced analytics. The connector can create a new table for the data, if it does not already exist.

- To provide access to Hadoop of the data stored in Vertica

- To allow Apache Pig to access data stored in Vertica

A MapReduce job that has to access data from Vertica executes a query to select its input. This query is passed into Hadoop's Map-Reduce API, the setInputMethod of the VerticaInputFormat class.

There are two ways one can use the query from the MapReduce job to get the input data from Vertica. The Vertica connector for MapReduce sends the query to Hadoop nodes, which individually connect to Vertica nodes to run the query and get their input data.

Queries can be in either of the following formats:

Self-contained query—VerticaInputFormat.setInput (job, "SELECT * FROM VerticaTable;");

Parameterized query with explicit parameters— VerticaInputFormat.setInput(job, "SELECT * FROM V WHERE ID = ?", "A", "B");

Vertica Hadoop Connector for HDFS

This connector is used by Vertica when HDFS acts as a source for an external table against which queries can be performed directly. This use case is needed when one needs to extract data from files that are periodically updated.

```
CREATE EXTERNAL TABLE HadoopFile(ID VARCHAR(10), Col1 INTEGER, Col2 INTEGER,
Col3 INTEGER) AS COPY SOURCE Hdfs(url='http://hadoopNameNode:50070/webhdfs/
user/User1/data/input/*',username='User1');
SELECT * FROM HadoopFile;
```

If you are looking for very fast low-latency analytics with SQL interface on large data sets that can reside either in a Vertica data store or on HDFS, Vertica's integration with Hadoop provides the right solution. However, keep in mind that Vertica is a commercial product whose pricing is based on the uncompressed data that is stored within its data store for analytical queries.

Vertica is not an open source product, and licensing costs of Vertica are charged at the amount of data ingested (before compression), apart from yearly maintenance costs. Vertica is a more mature product than any of the open source tools and technologies out there. Vertica also, if deployed correctly and set up correctly in terms of the projection tables, is blazingly fast with ad hoc SQL queries on large data sets.

Vertica's SQL compliance and support is richer and more complete, because it has been on the market for more than seven years. Vertica also supports a lot of advanced algorithms for some routine data-mining problems. Vertica is also very useful for doing star schema-based data warehouse queries. Vertica works well and has been battle-tested in its integration with most of the BI tools out there.

However, Vertica ideally requires its own dedicated cluster. If an organization already has a big data cluster, the provisioning and ongoing maintenance costs for Vertica can be prohibitive.

Jethro Data

One of the unique commercial SQL-on-Hadoop tools out there is Jethro. Jethro leverages the age-old technique of making queries run faster, using indexes. We are all so familiar with indexes in the world of databases, and with how they are used to speed up SQL queries in the relational world. So why did no one think about using indexes in the world of big data, to speed up queries? Well, Hive has had support for indexes for a while, although, to my knowledge, not too many real-world use cases and implementations have used it extensively.

The world of big data, especially HDFS, has a problem with indexes. Because HDFS is a WORM (write once read many [times]) kind of file system, keeping indexes updated as data is added and updated becomes a problem on HDFS. Indexes have had a minor role in speeding up queries in high-performance analytic databases and in big data implementations, owing to several reasons.

- Index data typically uses smaller block sizes, which are quite incompatible to the whole idea of bigger block sizes in the big data world.

- Index creation slows down data loads.

- With the addition of newer data, indexes have to be updated, which is, again, incompatible with the architecture of big data file systems such as HDFS and S3.

Jethro brings indexes into the world of big data SQL, by way of an innovative indexing mechanism to offset the aforementioned problems. Jethro's indexing mechanism is architected to work with HDFS/S3 and also solves the index update problem, using their architecture. Jethro's append-only index structure converts index updates to cheap sequential writes, solving the index update problem.

Jethro's solution fully indexes all columns in the data set and stores it on HDFS. Only the indexes are used to answer the query, instead of doing a full scan, as in the case of other MPP-based SQL-on-Hadoop solutions. The more a query drills down into a data set to get a finer level of detail, the better the performance gets, because indexes are leveraged to the best possible extent, unlike full-scan systems, which will do a full scan even for drilled-down queries. Index-based access to the data results in dramatically lowering the load on I/O and CPU and memory usage, as compared to MPP-based full-scan architectures.

When new data is added to the data set, Jethro architecture does not modify the existing indexes but adds the newer indexes at the end of the current indexes, allowing duplicate index entries. Instead of in-place updates of the index, the new index is appended to allow repeated values. An asynchronous process runs in the background, which merges the newer indexes with the older ones and removes the duplicates.

During the time frame when duplicate indexes exist in the system, the query executor will read multiple index fragments but makes sure to resolve the query results to the latest index values in case of duplicates.

The Jethro engine is installed on its own dedicated cluster, in which each node is stateless. This Jethro cluster is connected to either HDFS or S3, in which all the indexes are stored. Figure 4-17 shows the deployment architecture of Jethro.

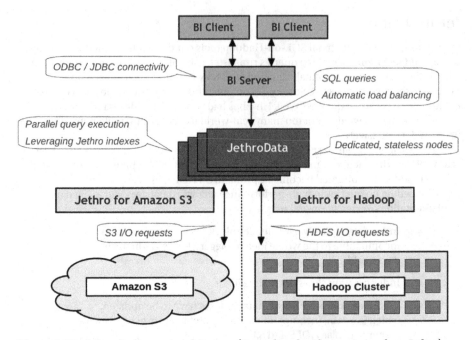

Figure 4-17. *Jethro deployment architecture (Reproduced with permission from Jethro)*

Apart from the regular speedup of accessing only the data needed for the query, Jethro has other performance-enhancing features, such as compressed columnar storage format of the index data, efficient skip scan I/O, automatic caching of locally frequently accessed column and index blocks. Jethro's query optimizer uses the index metadata to optimize the queries, rather than the usual statistics gathering and collection processes used in other systems.

Figure 4-18 shows the data flow of index creation during data ingestion and storage of the indexes on HDFS. These indexes are accessed by the Jethro cluster servers during query processing. The indexes are created synchronously as the data is ingested into the big data system.

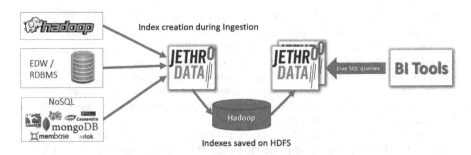

Figure 4-18. *Jethro data ingestion and query architecture (Reproduced with permission from Jethro)*

Jethro's execution engine is highly parallelized. The execution plan is made of many fine-grained operators, and the engine parallelizes the work within and across operators. The execution engine leverages query pipelining, whereby the rows are pipelined between operators, resulting in higher throughput and lower latency.

There are two downsides to Jethro's architecture:

1. A separate dedicated cluster of Jethro servers—separate from the Hadoop cluster—for hosting Jethro servers

2. A proprietary format of data, which is much faster than ORC/Parquet formats

The first downside is not a downside in the true sense, as it is always advisable to have separate clusters that support different workloads. Hadoop clusters meant for doing ETL and batch workloads should be separated from clusters that support real-time or interactive workloads to satisfy the SLAs. This separation of query clusters from other workload clusters results in better performance and the independent scalability of each cluster.

Others

There are a lot more products out there, but we cannot have full coverage to all of them. One product that has been gaining usage lately is Presto.

Presto has been developed at Facebook and is written completely in Java. It is very similar to Impala and Drill in terms of architecture and general concepts, though it is written in Java. However, compared to Impala or Drill, which have been on the market for a longer time, Presto is very new, although Netflix uses Presto extensively for ad hoc interactive analytics. Presto is an in-memory distributed SQL query engine that supports ANSI SQL and rich analytical functions. Presto is just the query engine; it is like Impala/Drill, not a storage engine. It can connect to a wide variety of data sources—relational, NoSQL, and distributed file systems.

Presto should not be used when you require batch processing or when one has to implement iterative machine-learning algorithms. Presto is also not recommended to use in data warehouses in which the dimensional modeling is done with star schemas.

MPP vs. Batch—Comparisons

We looked at Batch processing in last chapter, and in this chapter, we have focused on MPP-based architectures. Let's take some time to review the differences in architectures and the pros and cons of each from a purely architectural perspective and consider when to use which architectural solution.

MPP systems are different from SMP (symmetric multiprocessing). MPP systems are shared nothing architectures, that is, they eliminate usage of shared resources by processing units, with no SPOF (single point of failure) and hot swappable component architecture. These systems scale horizontally by adding nodes and scale queries by adding new nodes.

MPP architecture distributes data across many nodes (see Figure 4-19), and each node processes all of its local data for every query. It is a simple architecture that handles large aggregate queries well but requires many servers to be effective and consumes many resources per query across the cluster, limiting SQL concurrency. MPP architectures are designed to consume a significant portion of memory, CPU, and I/O bandwidth from every node in the cluster, for low latency.

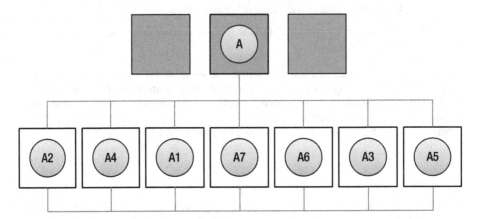

Figure 4-19. *MPP architecture distributes the work of a query across many nodes*

In an MPP-based architecture, each execution unit cannot access any resource from another execution unit. The only way for one execution unit to access data from another execution unit is through data exchange, using the network fabric. Each executor in an MPP architecture runs the same processing logic on its local data.

MPP architecture has some design problems, specifically problems associated when one of the executors becomes slow. It becomes the weakest link in the chain, a problem often called stragglers—tasks that are taking longer to finish than other tasks at the same stage. Under such circumstances, the performance characteristic of the whole system does not depend on the cluster size; it depends on the slowest node.

Performance of one or more nodes can degrade because of multiple reasons: perhaps a failed disk, failed memory, or any OS-level problems. Observations have led to the conclusion that at a certain scale, any MPP system would have a node with some problem, which would lead to degraded performance for the node, thereby limiting performance of the whole cluster.

Another major point to note for an MPP system is that because an MPP system is a perfectly symmetric system where each node is performing exactly the same task, all in parallel, the concurrency level of an MPP system is unrelated to the number of nodes in the cluster. Low concurrency of an MPP system, owing to the reasons previously stated, is the biggest trade-off users have to pay for extreme low latency.

In contrast to MPP systems, batch systems have multiple tasks running on each node in which the data resides. If the batch processing is based on HDFS, in case of node degradation, two solutions are attempted. Because HDFS is a file system with a default replication of three, tasks on one node can access the data on another data node across the network. Also, a speculative execution model allows the system to be resilient if one of the tasks is slow and is unable to keep pace with other tasks on other machines. Speculative execution is a mechanism used to guard against slow nodes in a cluster, by starting more tasks if a task fails to complete within some given SLAs. Speculative execution is not possible in an MPP system.

Speculative execution tries to solve the problem of stragglers. Speculative execution tries to run on some other executor a task that is not completing for any apparent reason. If the new task now happens to complete earlier than the original task that was not completing, a batch-based engine accepts the results of the new task and discards the old task. This avoids the problem of a single task holding up or slowing down the full execution.

In an MPP system, the intermediate data results are pipelined across the executors running on different nodes, while in a batch system, the intermediate results in the computations are stored on disk on the data nodes. This adds a huge amount of latency in batch-oriented systems. However, because batch systems are not shared nothing architectures, in the perfect sense, as are MPP systems, the scalability and concurrency of batch systems are much higher than in MPP systems, but with higher latency.

So, in short, batch-oriented systems have higher latency (bad) and higher concurrency (good), while MPP systems have low latency (good) and poor concurrency (bad). Whenever you evaluate an MPP system, make sure also to evaluate and benchmark it, based on your concurrency requirements.

Capabilities and Characteristics to Look for in the SQL Engine

In this last section of this chapter, we offer a brief look at some of the capabilities one should look out for when making a choice about the SQL engine. The following is by no means an exhaustive list, but it provides sufficient guidance and direction to make smart choices.

Technical Decisions

> *Latency*: Does the product support the kind of latency SLAs your business mandates? To make a decision requires careful consideration of the types of workloads, in addition to concurrency tests. The best way to approach this is to conduct a POC (proof of concept) of the product, with your data sets and the cluster size that your organization can support, and obtain realistic numbers from the POC. This is a very critical step, and it is always wise to do it for your data with your workloads, rather than just to trust the TPC benchmarks or the marketing materials of the product. One important point to remember when undertaking this POC is to make sure the product is tested for its latency at low, average, and worst-case concurrency levels, setting the expectations correctly.

Deployment modes: Does the product support the deployment models that your organization is comfortable with, whether they are cloud-, on-Premise-, or hybrid-based deployment models?

Data types: Does the product support all the data types that are part of the data sets within your organization?

Data formats: Does the product support the data formats that are currently being used in your data pipelines and ETL processes? If this is not the case, new ETL has to be written to convert the data formats, and this could entail missing the SLAs.

Data sources: Does the product work with all the data sources—streaming, files, directories, NoSQL, NewSQL, RDBMS, and mainframes—data sources that your organization relies on as raw data sources?

Dependence on HDFS: Does the product rely on Hadoop-based components, such as working with HDFS? Verifying this ensures that your organization is not adding accidental complexity to the overall deployments just to satisfy the requirements of the product you are selecting.

Schema requirements: Does the engine require schema definition up front, or can the schema be defined on read?

Query language support: This is a very important decision point. What type of query support does the engine offer out of the box, and does it satisfy the minimum query support criteria required for the system your organization is building?

UDF/UDAF/UDTF support: To the preceding point, is it possible to build out unsupported features or functionality using UDFs, UDAFs, UDTFs, and the language in which these functionalities can be developed?

Support triggers: Does the system support triggers for alerts and notifications as a typical RDBMS would do, if this is an important criterion for your organization and workflows?

Security: What are the minimum security requirements, in terms of data encryption for data at rest, data in motion, and authentication and authorization policies and ACLs permitted by the system in consideration, and do they match what your current organizational policies are.

Concurrency: This is a very important consideration, in addition to that of latency. Understanding how the concurrency affects latency and the workload and whether the engine can be made scalable by adding more nodes with increasing concurrency must be thoroughly examined, and the system tuned, to get the best performance.

Compression: It is important to understand what kind of compression formats are supported by the engine and what the pros and cons of each of them are. Also important to evaluate are the performance characteristics of the engine for some of the chosen compression formats that are to be used by your organization.

Secondary indexes: Most SQL engines do not support secondary indexes from an architecture perspective. Depending on your use cases and your data, it is wise to include in your POC workloads that which would perform better with secondary index support. Then you should evaluate the performances of the engines without secondary index support and compare the trade-offs.

Massive table join: Most MPP engines shy away or do not perform too well with joins across massive tables on a distributed platform. However, there could be cases in your organization in which you will require them. There are multiple ways to avoid this, but in the case where it cannot be avoided, it is best to learn the gotchas and test the robustness and latency of the SQL engine in consideration of such massive joins.

Optimizers: This is an internal component of most SQL engines, over which the end user has no control. However, it is still best to understand the kind of optimizations that the SQL engine would achieve for the different workloads that your use cases require.

Performance tuning: Before selecting an SQL engine, it is vital to know the kinds of performance tuning knobs and controls available to the end user, to improve performance and identify the bottlenecks and how they can be avoided.

Data import/export capabilities: It is important to know the different ways of ingesting and exporting data from the SQL engines and the latencies associated with them, making sure that the processes are acceptable and the latencies are within the SLA bounds of your organization.

Data locality: How does the engine under consideration handle data locality issues? Does it totally disregard it, but still perform very well? This becomes especially important when these engines are deployed on the cloud.

Hardware: The kind of hardware platform—in terms of CPU, memory, I/O and networking capabilities—that the SQL engine recommends for best practices and most optimum performance is an important consideration from budgetary, data growth and scalability perspectives.

Fault tolerance: Questions such as how is fault tolerance achieved by the architecture of the engine and its components are very important to consider clearly, in order to provide reliability and uptime-related metrics and SLAs to the end customers who are relying on the SQL engine for their activities.

CLI/API/ODBC/JDBC: What kind of APIs (REST) and driver support does the SQL engine have to connect with external applications? This may be a non-blocking issue in terms of the product selection, but an important consideration when selecting the SQL engine of choice.

Tool support: Understanding the tooling support—admin, monitoring, maintenance, troubleshooting, data ingestion— of the SQL engine is very important for debugging and troubleshooting purposes, as well as for regular automation, monitoring, and admin-related functionalities.

Soft Decisions

Maturity: When choosing an SQL engine for big data processing, it is very important to reach a decision based on the maturity of the product and its adoption rate, etc. A lot of new products come to the market and then fizzle out and do not have enough tracking, backing by investors/committers who could work on the product. Newer products go through a lot of changes in the initial stages of product development and require time to mature and become robust for industrial-scale data loads and performance.

Customer base: Evaluating the customer base and typical things those customers are doing with the SQL engine offer a good perspective on the quality of the product, its capabilities, shortcomings, best practices, and best usage scenarios.

License: Understanding fully the licensing model is always helpful, keeping in mind future growth, both from hardware and licensing perspectives.

Source code: It is also important to understand the nature of the source code of the product and if that is something that can be changed/contributed to by your organization, in case of bug fixes or adding new capabilities, etc. Understanding in what language the product has been written is also equally important, because it determines if your organization has the necessary skillset in case some things have to be changed or modified at the code level.

Roadmap: As with any product evaluation, it is important to understand the roadmap and vision of the particular SQL engine you have chosen. You must be aware of its release cycle and also of how the product addresses the most commonly asked questions and customer concerns.

Summary

This chapter covered a lot of ground, exploring the architecture and internals of many interactive features of SQL on big data engines. This is a vast area, with lots of related products on the market, which often causes difficulty in making the right choice as to which product is best for different workloads and different use cases.

The final section of this chapter covered the criteria to follow in order to select the right product and make the right decisions.

CHAPTER 5

■ ■ ■

SQL for Streaming, Semi-Structured, and Operational Analytics

This chapter is divided into three major topics: SQL on semi-structured data, SQL on streaming data, and SQL for operational analytics on big data platforms. It covers the technologies for each of the preceding areas in which SQL can be applied in big data systems. Because of the ubiquity, ease of understanding, and available skill set of SQL, rather than designing a new way to query and access data irrespective of its origin, mode of availability, or format, SQL is being increasingly used as the way to access these data sets. New tools and frameworks are being developed today with this in mind, and at the same time, existing tools and frameworks are being morphed to ensure that they accept SQL as the lingua franca for any of these data types.

SQL on Semi-Structured Data

Though not evident, unstructured data comprises most of the data we deal with on a daily basis. It has been found that the majority of the data in an enterprise is unstructured data, in the form of e-mails, blogs, wiki, documents, and so on. In the past, most of this unstructured data lay unused, primarily for two reasons: lack of tools to support easy access, manipulation, and querying of this data, and the inability of a lot of enterprises to figure out good business use cases to make this data valuable and useful. However, this has changed dramatically over the last couple of years. With the digital revolution and most of the web data being available in JSON format, more and more organizations want to use this untapped data for building products that provide data-driven insights and leverage unstructured data sets for building newer products and improving the quality of existing ones.

With increased adoption by enterprises and organizations of both unstructured and semi-structured data sets, the onus is now on the products, tools, and frameworks to provide ways to access the semi-structured data in a seamless way. This access becomes even more seamless if existing tools and applications in an enterprise can obtain the semi-structured data by using SQL, which is deeply embedded within most organizations.

© Sumit Pal 2016
S. Pal, *SQL on Big Data*, DOI 10.1007/978-1-4842-2247-8_5

In this section, we will cover some of the existing products, such as Apache Drill and Apache Spark, which have adapted to this trend from the very beginning, and how they have been architected and evolved to support SQL over semi-structured data sets.

Apache Drill—JSON

Apache Drill has been architected with the idea of building an SQL engine for everything, i.e., applying SQL query semantics to any form of data, residing anywhere, whether in files or databases that are structured or semi-structured. Apache Drill has very powerful capabilities to work with JSON data, and it infers the schema automatically. Drill can perform SQL directly on files and directories, without requiring any schema definitions.

For example, Apache Drill can do the following SQL query on JSON data out of the box, on a file that contains JSON data:

```
Select field1, field2, ... from <path to JSON file> where field2 like '%me%'
```

The best part of Apache Drill is that it can seamlessly join different datasets, each of which can reside either in raw files/directories/RDBMS/NoSQL data stores/Hive, etc.

Unlike Apache Spark, which, you will see later, requires that the JSON data be in one line for it to be queried, Drill has no such restriction.

Some Examples of Querying JSON Data with Apache Drill

If you have a JSON key such as the one below

```
group:
[
  [1,2,3],

  [4,5,6],

  [7,8,9]
]
```

```
Select group[1][2] ...
```

will return 5

If you have a JSON file as below

```
{
    "id": "0001",
    "type": "pizza",
    "name": "NYStyle",
    "ppu": 0.1,
    "sales": 50,
```

```
"batters":
  {
    "batter":
      [
        { "id": "1", "type": "Regular" },
        { "id": "2", "type": "Chilli" }
      ]
  },
  "topping":
    [
      { "id": "1", "type": "None" },
      { "id": "2", "type": "Eggplant" },
      { "id": "3", "type": "Pepper" },
      { "id": "4", "type": "Olives" },
      { "id": "5", "type": "Onion" },
      { "id": "6", "type": "Pineapple" },
      { "id": "7", "type": "Chicken" }
    ]
}
```

```
select topping[3] as top from pizza.json
```

will return {"id": "4", "type": "Olives"}.

```
select t.topping[3].id as record, t.topping[3].type as type from pizza.json
as t
```

will return

```
+------------+---------------+
|   record   | type          |
+------------+---------------+
| 4          | Olives        |
+------------+---------------+
```

All data in Apache Drill is internally represented as a JSON data structure, which aids Drill in discovering the schema on the fly. This idea is extremely powerful and allows Drill to query complex data models that change the structure dynamically. This makes Apache Drill ideal for working with unstructured and semi-structured data sets.

Flatten and KVGEN are two useful functions in Apache Drill that work with JSON data. We discuss this in the next two sections.

FLATTEN

FLATTEN is a UDF (user defined function) available out of the box in Drill. It is useful to represent repeated data typically found in JSON data formats in a more structured and easier way.

FLATTEN is typically used in arrays in JSON data, to break them up into multiple rows. Let's say you have a data row from JSON which is like this:

```
{
  "Name":"Workbar",
  "Location":["Cambridge", "Arlington", "Boston", "Needham"]
}
```

With the FLATTEN function, as used in the following example, you get something like this:

```
select Name, flatten(locations) as location from workbar_business.json
```

This will return the following:

```
+-------------+-------------+
|    Name     | Locations   |
+-------------+-------------+
| Workbar     | Cambridge   |
| Workbar     | Arlington   |
| Workbar     | Boston      |
| Workbar     | Needham     |
+-------------+-------------+
```

KVGEN

KVGEN is applied to JSON data when, within the JSON files, there are arbitrary maps consisting of unknown or unspecified column names. This is very typical of semi-structured data. Rather than specifying keys (columns) in the map to access the data, KVGEN can return a list of keys in the map. Essentially, it transposes a map with a wide set of columns into an array of key-value pairs. See the example below for more clarity.

If we have a JSON file that has data such as the following:

```
{"Row":{"1": "A", "2": "B"}}
{"Row":{"3": "C", "4": "D"}}
{"Row":{"5": "E", "6": "F"}}
```

running this SQL: `select KVGEN (row) from file.json` will return the data as

```
[{"key":"1","value":"A"},{"key":"2","value":"B"}]
[{"key":"3","value":"C"},{"key":"4","value":"D"}]
[{"key":"5","value":"E"},{"key":"6","value":"F"}]
```

Now, if we apply the FLATTEN operation to the preceding, we get a structure as following code example.

select `FLATTEN(KVGEN(row))` from `file.json` will return the data as in the following code, which seems more structured and meaningful.

```
{"key": "1", "value": "A"}
{"key": "2", "value": "B"}
{"key": "3", "value": "C"}
{"key": "4", "value": "D"}
{"key": "5", "value": "E"}
{"key": "6", "value": "F"}
```

Apache Drill—XML

XML is another data format used widely to represent semi-structured data. However, JSON is considered a much slimmer version of XML. We will not cover too many of the capabilities of Apache Drill with XML data. However, if you have XML data and would like to use Apache Drill, here is the way to go about doing it. Drill supports XML by converting XML to JSON format. A SAX-based XML to JSON parser can generate JSON-compatible code to work with Drill, using the JSON parsing capabilities.

Apache Spark—JSON

Spark SQL has supported JSON since Spark version 1.1, and it has continuously kept improving its support. Spark SQL is capable of loading data from a variety of data sources, including plain JSON files. However, one of the constraints of using Spark SQL with JSON is that the JSON file must be such that it has one line for the full JSON object. This can be achieved with some tools and some code, but in order to use Spark SQL on JSON, the JSON file cannot be in the pretty format we see when we open a JSON file in a text editor in which we have line breaks and tabs to make the JSON file readable by humans.

Internally, JSON parsing in Spark SQL uses Jackson's ObjectMapper. It is easy and fast, but it requires two things to work: JSON data and the Java class that describes the schema. Spark infers the schema of a JSON file internally, using the parser, and using a Map-based data structure, it converts Jackson's data types to Spark's own data types. For this to work reliably, each line of this file should contain a separate, self-contained, valid JSON object.

Internally, it uses a `TextInputFormat`, which is a predefined file input format in Spark to parse text files. The following code in Spark with Scala demonstrates how easy it is to use JSON data with SQL semantics using the Spark framework.

Let us look at the following simple example. It shows the JSON data we have, which is nested one level deep.

```
{"firstName": "First_AA", "lastName": "Last_AA", "age": 35, "address":
{"state": "WA", "postalCode": "30021"}}
{"firstName": "First_BB", "lastName": "Last_BB", "age": 40, "address":
{"state": "MA", "postalCode": "40345"}}
{"firstName": "First_CC", "lastName": "Last_CC", "age": 65, "address":
{"state": "VA", "postalCode": "64321"}}
{"firstName": "First_DD", "lastName": "Last_DD", "age": 20, "address":
{"state": "TX", "postalCode": "02345"}}
```

The code to infer the schema automatically by Spark is

```
val fileName = "test.json"
val testJSONDF = spark.read.json(path)
testJSONDF.printSchema()
```

This results in the following:

```
root
 |-- address: struct (nullable = true)
 |    |-- postalCode: string (nullable = true)
 |    |-- state: string (nullable = true)
 |-- age: long (nullable = true)
 |-- firstName: string (nullable = true)
 |-- lastName: string (nullable = true)
```

This is the code to run a simple SQL query against the data set:

```
testJSONDF.createOrReplaceTempView("test")
val query1DF = spark.sql("SELECT * FROM test WHERE age BETWEEN 20 AND 40")
query1DF.show()
```

The results are as follows:

```
+-----------+---+---------+--------+
|    address|age|firstName|lastName|
+-----------+---+---------+--------+
|[30021,WA]| 35| First_AA| Last_AA|
|[40345,MA]| 40| First_BB| Last_BB|
|[02345,TX]| 20| First_DD| Last_DD|
+-----------+---+---------+--------+
```

```
val query2DF = spark.sql("SELECT * FROM test WHERE test.address.state like
'TX'")
query2DF.show()
```

Further results follow:

```
+-----------+---+---------+--------+
|    address|age|firstName|lastName|
+-----------+---+---------+--------+
|[02345,TX]| 20| First_DD| Last_DD|
+-----------+---+---------+--------+
```

More complex SQL with aggregations and window-based functions can be applied to the data set thus derived from JSON data. Very large JSON data sets can be easily parsed at scale, and SQL queries run over them, using Spark SQL's native interface to work with JSON data using SQL.

At an architectural level, this is what happens under the hood, as shown in Figure 5-1.

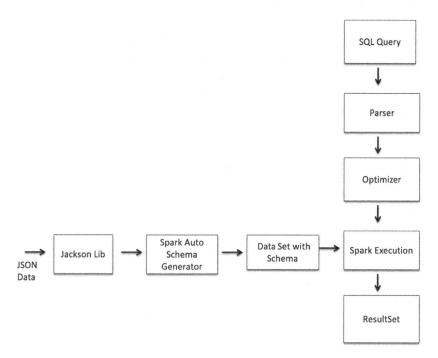

Figure 5-1. *JSON data processing in Spark*

Apache Spark—Mongo

In this section, we will briefly discuss how Apache Spark can work with MongoDB. MongoDB is best suited to natively storing JSON/BSON (Binary JSON) data. You will see how Spark SQL can work with data stored in MongoDB with JSON data.

Ideally, MongoDB is meant to store data for content-management systems or product catalog data with hierarchies or operational data. It has a flexible JSON-based data model, which allows dynamic schema modifications. Spark, on the other hand, is a highly scalable data-processing framework. With Spark's ability to read any data source in any format, it becomes ideal to leverage Spark SQL to query and work with JSON data residing in a Mongo database.

There exists an open source MongoDB to Spark connector developed by a company called Stratio based out of Spain. MongoDB connector is a plug-in for Spark that provides the ability to use MongoDB as an input/output source for jobs running in either Spark/ Hadoop-based frameworks. The Stratio connector to Spark supports SQL queries on Mongo data. This is exposed as a data source that implements the Spark DataFrame API. Internally, this connector API implements a `PrunedFilterScan` algorithm rather than a plain vanilla `TableScan`, because MongoDB supports secondary indexes on its data. The connector API infers the schema, by sampling documents from the MongoDB collection, and internally uses Spark's Catalyst optimizer for both rule-based and cost-based optimizations.

The following sample Code shows how Spark SQL can be used to connect to a Mongo data source and how data is queried using SQL syntax:

```
// Import the relevant implicits classes and packages from Stratio

val mongoConnectionBuilder = MongodbConfigBuilder(Map(Host ->
List("HOSTNAME:PORT#"), Database -> "DBName", Collection ->
"mongoColletionName", SamplingRatio -> 1.0, WriteConcern ->
MongodbWriteConcern.Normal))

val connection = mongoConnectionBuilder.build()

val sparkToMongo = sqlContext.fromMongoDB(connection)    //set up the MongoDB
collection to read from as a DataFrame
//make a pointer to the collection from Spark as register it as a temp table
sparkToMongo.registerTempTable("MongoCollectionAsSparkTable")

// Valid SQL query to query JSON from Mongo
val dataFrame = sqlContext.sql("SELECT columns* FROM
MongoCollectionAsSparkTable")
dataFrame.show
```

Other document databases, such as Couchbase, also provide similar connectors to leverage the power of Spark SQL with semi-structured data sets.

SQL on Streaming Data

With the rapid rise of the IOT (Internet of Things) and cybersecurity, support for SQL on data in motion—streaming data or fast data—has become a necessity in most tools and frameworks. Stream processing has taken off in the big data world in a big way. Various products, both in the commercial and open source spaces, are trying to add an SQL interface for streaming data analysis.

SQL for stream processing will make streaming technology accessible to a wider audience. It will also enable development of new use cases, as interactive and ad hoc stream analysis, and simplify applications that use data in motion to perform real-time analytics.

We will explore streaming SQL capabilities available in the Spark framework and a new database called PipelineDB. In addition, we will look at Apache Calcite, an evolving framework defining the standards for correct SQL syntax and semantics for supporting SQL on streams.

Traditionally, SQL is applied on stored data. However, the idea of first storing the data and then doing the queries falls apart with streaming data. Streams can be considered to be infinitely long tables. The idea of doing SQL on streaming data is flipped, as compared to doing SQL on static data. For SQL on streaming data, the data flows while the queries are static, meaning that the queries that have to be executed on the data are generally predetermined. Compared to the traditional way of doing SQL, the data is static—stored on the disk/memory, while the end user or applications access this data with ad hoc SQL queries.

Because streaming data is fleeting and has associated velocity, Hadoop, which was designed mainly for batch operations, is unable to offer latency and throughput for real-time applications such as telecom, cybersecurity, and IOT. The general approach while implementing SQL on streaming data is to continuously operate on the data as it arrives and store the computed results into a data store for future access.

Because the concept of store and then compute does not apply for streaming data, most streaming SQL engine architectures employ in-memory processing capabilities, along with usage of lock-free data structures, and use stateless implementations that enable queries to be distributed over nodes in the cluster.

Apache Spark

Batch data can be thought of as a snapshot of streaming data. This is what Apache Spark leverages in order to support SQL on streaming data. Spark has inherently been architected to be an in-memory batch-processing system. However, to implement streaming capabilities with Spark, it uses the concept of micro-batches, in which the batch size is reduced to accommodate smaller windows of processing time. In other words, Spark streaming takes incoming data that arrives at some time periods and repackages them as RDDs (Resilient Distributed Datasets) or data frames or data sets.

Spark streaming brings in the concept of DStreams—Discretized Streams—in which computations are structured as a series of stateless, deterministic batch computations at small-time intervals called windows. Each such DStream contains a series of RDDs that are processed as a unit. A DStream is defined when a StreamingContext, in Spark parlance, is defined with two parameters (refer to Figure 5-2).

1. Window of data (from the infinite data stream that is coming in), at which the processing is going to look

2. Amount of units, by which the window is to be slided, to get the next data set for processing

There are two important concepts to understand when talking about DStreams in Spark streaming, as shown in Figure 5-2.

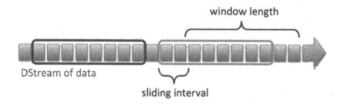

Figure 5-2. Window and sliding interval for DStream

1. Windows: Operation, which groups all the records from a sliding window of past time intervals into one data unit to be processed at a time

2. State: How to preserve the computations made in an earlier window and how to apply the previously computed results to the next DStream to calculate the new results

The basic idea of applying SQL on streaming data in Spark can be easily explained if we look at Figure 5-3.

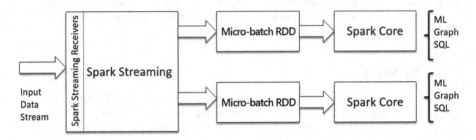

Figure 5-3. *High-level spark streaming architecture*

Delving one layer deeper, Figure 5-4 shows what happens after the streaming data comes into the Spark framework and how to apply Spark SQL on the data streams (DStream).

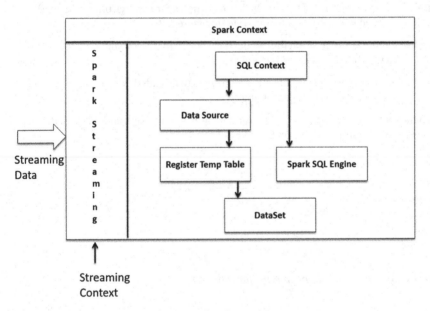

Figure 5-4. *Spark streaming integrated with Spark SQL components*

The basic idea is that Spark streaming splits the streaming data into time-based mini-batches, called the DStream, which internally are RDDs.

Following is an outline of the set of steps required in a Spark streaming application in which Spark SQL is to be used to work with DStreams.

1. Define the Spark StreamingContext with the window size.

2. Define the data source that identifies the streaming data, which could be files, sockets, or a message bus.

3. Wrap the source with the StreamingContext.

4. Create the DStream by defining the window and slider sizes.

5. For each DStream, get the RDDs, and for each such RDD, create the Spark DataFrame or DataSet object.

6. Register the DataFrame or DataSet as a temporary table.

7. Start using SQL queries on the DataFrame or DataSet as one would use them for a normal data set.

PipelineDB

In this section, we will take a quick look at a new upcoming database called Pipeline DB and some of its streaming SQL capabilities. As the name suggests, it is a database that works continuously on streaming incoming data.

PipelineDB is a relational database that runs SQL queries continuously on streaming data and stores incremental results in tables. PipelineDB provides a continuous view of the desired calculations (specified using SQL operations), updating results continuously. The continuous update of the results is achieved by seamlessly integrating the previous computed results with the latest results.

Traditional databases store the data on disk first, before it becomes ready for querying. PipelineDB flips the order by first doing the query and then storing the results. It is important to understand the rationale behind this. Streaming data often arrives at a high velocity, and there is not enough time to store the data, read it, and then apply analytics or do a computation. In order to reduce latency, the analytics and computation have to be done as the data streams in.

The original data can be either thrown away or stored, depending on the end application use cases. PipelineDB makes streaming analytics possible with pure SQL. You can think of PipelineDB as doing continuous SQL on streaming data, with incremental materialized views. Under the covers, PipelineDB uses Postgres.

However, PipelineDB is most useful when queries are known in advance. It is not meant to perform ad hoc SQL queries on streaming data. The outputs of PipelineDB can be explored in an ad hoc manner, but ad hoc SQL queries cannot be performed using PipelineDB.

PipelineDB has three primitive operations: continuous view, continuous transform, and continuous trigger.

Continuous View

A continuous view is a view over continuously flowing data.

A continuous view looks like the following: CREATE CONTINUOUS VIEW V AS
<A SQL Query>, where SQL Query is a subset of Postgres-based SQL syntax with
windowing capabilities.

Following is an example of a continuous view with a condition:

```
CREATE CONTINUOUS VIEW V WITH (window = '1 day') AS
SELECT COUNT (*) FROM stream
```

Continuous Transform

Continuous transform applies an end-user-specified transform to an event in the
incoming data and creates a new transformed stream.

```
CREATE CONTINUOUS TRANSFORM T AS query THEN EXECUTE PROCEDURE function
```

Continuous Trigger

Continuous trigger is a trigger that fires when a condition becomes true in a continuous
view, as in the following example:

```
CREATE TRIGGER X ON VIEW WHEN Condition (Value)
```

Continuous Aggregate

Continuous Aggregate computes the aggregates (PipelineDB has a rich set of aggregate
and windowing functions) and incrementally updates the results in real time as new data
streams arrive. PipelineDB ships with a plethora of aggregate functions, some of which
are based on approximate probabilistic data structures such as Bloom Filters, T-Digest,
HyperLogLog, and Count-Min Sketch, to name a few.

PipelineDB has the following kind of flow:

> Buffer the Streaming Data ➤ Query the Microbatch ➤
> Incrementally Update the Table

PipelineDB has been built to support some of the most commonly used analytic
functions: COUNT, DISTINCT, Top-K, Percentiles.

Apache Calcite

Apache Calcite, originally called Apache Optiq, is built to provide a framework for performing SQL query optimization. Any SQL engine will have to do query optimization, based on numerous rules and cost models and I/O, CPU time, or data shuffling time. Calcite provides the libraries, so that SQL optimization can be provided out of the box by the Calcite engine once metadata is provided to Calcite.

So, why was a product like Calcite conceived? All SQL engines use an SQL optimizer to optimize the SQL queries. This optimization is needed to reduce the latency as well as to prevent unnecessary use of system resources, thus indirectly helping with latency and concurrency. These optimizers are invisible to the end user who issues the query and impatiently waits for the results. Internally, these optimizers are complex engines that use cost metrics such as– amount of I/O and disk access, amount of CPU cycles, and amount of memory consumed to run the query. These optimizers use rule-based algorithms to rewrite the original SQL query, so that it returns the same results but performs lesser work in doing so. Internally, these optimizers use data profiling and data statistics to prepare the best query execution plan, which optimizes the resource usage and minimizes the time it takes to return the query results.

Over a period of time, it was found that these optimizers across most SQL engines essentially do the same task. Hence, the idea for Calcite was, rather than to reinvent the wheel by building in hard-coded specific rules to perform SQL optimization within each SQL Engine, to reuse SQL optimization capabilities across multiple SQL engines.

Calcite can also be called a data management framework—one which is used in creating databases—but Calcite ignores solving all the problems associated with building databases. It does not focus on storage, metadata, or the internal algorithms used for data processing. By doing this, Calcite becomes the glue layer that brings together the different pieces needed to build a database. Calcite provides an abstraction to create federated data architectures. It is not a database but provides a way to access the data in the data stores, using adapters.

With Apache Calcite, data stored in any data store, whether NoSQL, files (any format), or streams, can be accessed using SQL. With the rapid development of SQL on top of streaming solutions, each tool is bringing to market its own extensions to the SQL language, to accommodate stream processing primitives to its processing engine. What Apache Calcite is trying to do is to build a standard set of streaming SQL query primitives that can be parsed and optimized and then passed on to the SQL engine and its data store for processing. This is done in accordance with the adapter pattern principle in software engineering, by developing adapters that work with Calcite and the SQL engine in question.

Figure 5-5 offers a snapshot of Calcite's high-level architecture.

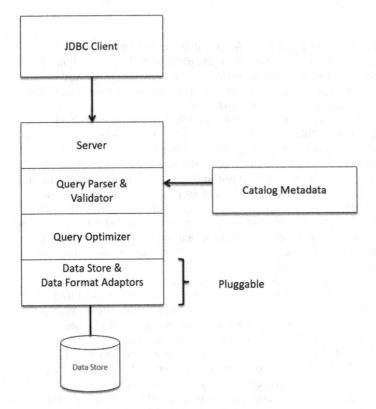

Figure 5-5. *Apache Calcite high-level architecture*

Calcite has extended SQL and relational algebra to support SQL on streaming data. This streaming SQL is easy and very implicit.

```
SELECT [STREAM] [ALL | DISTINCT]
       { * | projectItem [, projectItem ]* }
    FROM tableExpression
    [ WHERE booleanExpression ]
    [ GROUP BY { groupItem [, groupItem ]* } ]
    [ HAVING booleanExpression ]
    [ WINDOW windowName AS windowSpec [, windowName AS windowSpec ]* ]
```

The sections in **boldface** are the extensions added by Calcite for SQL on streaming support.

The STREAM keyword is the main extension in streaming SQL. It tells the system that the source of data is the stream.

With this SQL syntax, one can use a table as a stream and vice versa. This is a very powerful concept, because now, one can execute SQL both from stream and from static table and do essentially what lambda architecture tries to do, by mixing and matching both past data as well as fast data (fresh streaming data) to give consolidated results. This allows end results to have both the data from short-term history as well as long-term history. It also allows one to join a data from a stream to a static table, or join a stream with another stream.

Streaming SQL query support has to have very strong support for windowing-based queries, which in the streaming world use the time dimension heavily. Apache Calcite supports three types of windowing queries:

1. Tumbling Windows: Every "N" seconds emits the results of the computation for "N" seconds.

    ```
    Select Stream ... from Table group by tumble(rowtimestamp,
    "interval N Time Units")
    ```

2. Hopping Windows: Every "N1" seconds emits the results of the computation for "N2" seconds.

    ```
    Select Stream ... from Table group by hop(rowtimestamp, "interval
    N1 Time Units", "interval N2 Time Units")
    ```

3. Sliding Window: For every record emits the results of the computation for "N" surrounding records.

SQL for Operational Analytics on Big Data Platforms

Hadoop was invented to do batch analytics on large data sets. These data sets were read-only, and Hadoop's major component HDFS was a write once read many (WORM) file system. Use cases or workloads that would entail use of these systems for updates, deletes, etc., were never part of the initial features Hadoop was meant to address.

Realistically, however, the success of a platform usually has had the effect of demanding more from it. This is why the industry began to explore the idea of having Hadoop, big data tools, and frameworks dispatch transactional workloads typically executed on operational systems. In this section of the chapter, we will take a look at some of the new tools in the landscape that are trying to address this use case and build new systems and databases, and ways to solve this problem on a big data platform. In Chapter 6, we will also look at the Hybrid Transactional and Analytics Platform (HTAP), which is a unified platform that supports both operational and analytical workloads. Development of systems capable of executing operational workloads within a big data ecosystem represents a step in the right direction.

In Chapter 3, we looked at how newer versions of Hive, starting from version 0.14, support transactional SQL capabilities, and this helps to support operational workloads. This was just the starting point that fueled industry leaders and innovators to delve further into supporting this, by building newer systems. "Operational" capabilities is an emerging Hadoop market category and, therefore, one of the least mature, stable, and robust, but the tools in this space are rapidly evolving and getting used in real production environments.

111

Transactional workloads are always mission-critical for business, because they represent their bread and butter and touch points for customers. Hence, handling operational workloads has very strict SLAs in terms of response times, transactional guarantees, data integrity, concurrency, and availability.

The different types of workloads, with their latency requirements, are shown in Figure 5-6.

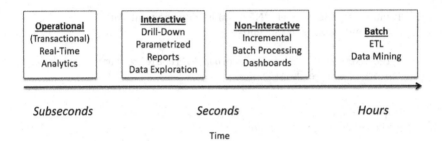

Figure 5-6. Workloads and their typical latencies

Trafodion

Trafodion is one of the first big data systems we explore and delve deeper into to see how it addresses operational capabilities on a big data system. It is an open source product, initiated by HP Labs, to develop an enterprise-level SQL-on-Hadoop engine that targets transactional and operational workloads. Under the covers, Trafodion builds on the capabilities of Hadoop, such as scalability, availability, replication, and parallel processing, but does not reinvent the wheel.

Following is a list of some of the major features of Trafodion:

It is a fully functional ANSI SQL DBMS with support for the syntax and semantics of INSERT/DELETE/UPDATE/MERGE, etc.

It extends HBase by adding transactional support with ACID semantics.

It has an extensive list of built-in optimizations for low-latency SQL, both for read and write operations.

It provides standard JDBC and ODBC drivers for third-party applications to connect and interact with it.

It provides a relational schema abstraction on top of HBase, which makes it feel like working with any other relational database and makes transition to HBase much easier.

It supports creating and managing database objects such as schemas, tables, views, stored procedures, and constraints. It supports referential integrity and not-null, unique, and primary-key based constraints.

It has the transactional support found in most relational databases, such as BEGIN WORK, COMMIT WORK, ROLLBACK WORK, SET TRANSACTIONS, etc.

It provides security privileges with operators such as GRANT/REVOKE.

It provides a plethora of utilities, such as Update Statistics, Explain, Command Line Interface, Bulk Loader, Backup and Restore, etc., found in most typical RDBMS.

In spite of being built on top of HBase, Trafodion innovates in multiple areas and provides the following capabilities:

- It has the ability to define Primary Keys, which can be simple or composite.

- It supports secondary indexes (which HBase does not).

- It adds a broader scope of ACID over HBase and allows transactions to span over multiple SQL statements, tables, and rows.

- It defines data types for columns, though HBase treats any stored data as an array of bytes.

Architecture

In this section, we will look at the core architectural underpinnings of Trafodion. Trafodion is not a storage engine per se but an SQL execution engine that leverages HBase and, hence, Hadoop and HDFS, under the covers. We will first look at how Trafodion fits the scheme of things within the Hadoop ecosystem and then take a look a level deeper into the architecture of the Trafodion engine.

Trafodion is designed to build upon and leverage Apache Hadoop and HBase core modules. Trafodion extensively uses HDFS and Zookeeper, the tow vital cogs within the Hadoop ecosystem. Internally, Trafodion interacts with HDFS, HBase, and Zookeeper, using Java-based APIs. Trafodion leverages the scalability, elasticity, and availability aspects of Hadoop and leverages parallel performance, load balancing across regions of data available from HBase and weaving the two together to form a true transactional processing system on the big data platform.

Figure 5-7 shows how Trafodion fits into the Hadoop ecosystem.

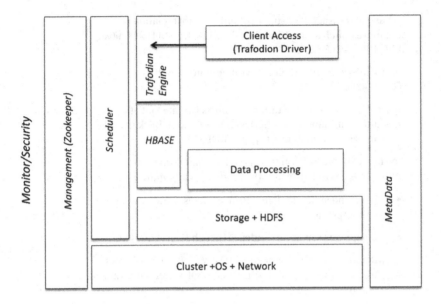

Figure 5-7. *Trafodion and the Hadoop ecosystem*

Trafodion adds its own ODBC and JDBC drivers for third-party tools and APIs. It also adds its own SQL engine, which sits atop HBase and HDFS and adds a Distributed Transaction Manager module to coordinate transactions within the database.

Trafodion is architected in three distinct layers: Client, SQL, and Storage layers.

> *Client layer*: This allows connectivity to third-party applications, tools, and BI engines, using standard ODBC/JDBC drivers. It supports both Type 2 and Type 4 JDBC drivers.
>
> *SQL layer*: This consists of the services for managing the different database-related objects and operations. It includes basic services such as connection management, SQL compilation and generation and execution of execution plans, and transaction and workload management.
>
> *Storage layer*: This is the set of services Trafodion requires from HDFS and HBase to store and manage the different database objects. On this layer, Trafodion maps the standard SQL queries and operational/transaction semantics to native HBase API calls. Trafodion can manage data residing in Hive and HBase—labeled as external data.

At a very high level, Trafodion's architecture looks as shown in Figure 5-8.

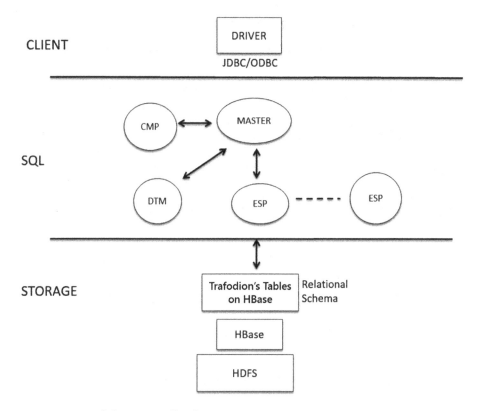

Figure 5-8. *Trafodion—overall architecture*

Upon request for a client connection, Trafodion's database connection service, which resides in the SQL layer, processes the request and assigns the connection to a Trafodion Master process residing in the SQL layer. Zookeeper (not shown in the diagram) internally manages all the connections in coordination with the connection service.

Master process is the entry point for all SQL queries. On receipt of a DML query, the Master process hands over the query to the CMP (compiler and optimizer process), which checks to see if the query result or the query plan is cached and, if not, parses, compiles, and generates the optimized query execution plan. The query is then fanned out to all or one (depending on whether the query is to be handled in parallel) to the ESP residing in each of the region server nodes (Executive Service Processes), to perform the actual work of executing the query. The ESP process coordinates with the storage engine to fetch the data from the data store in the most optimized way and also works with the Storage layer to push down the query predicates.

Finally, when all the ESPs have returned the query results, the Master process assembles all the fragments of query results and returns the result to the Client layer. In the event that parallel processing of the data by the ESPs is not required (depending on the type of the query), the Master process interacts directly with the HBase API to do the work and get the results.

How Trafodion Handles Transactions

HBase by itself offers transaction boundaries across only a single row. When transactional guarantees are required across tables, or multiple rows, HBase falls short. This is where Trafodion takes HBase to the next level, by supporting transactions across multiple rows and across multiple tables residing across any region server. Trafodion does this using a two-phase commit protocol. Transaction protection is automatically propagated across Trafodion components and processes.

Trafodion added a brand-new HBase distributed transaction management (DTM) subsystem for distributed transaction processing across multiple HBase regions. DTM provides both implicit (auto-commit) and explicit (BEGIN, COMMIT, ROLLBACK WORK) transaction control boundaries. Trafodion also leverages MVCC features, which are built-in within HBase to allow some of the transactional semantics such as read committed and conflict resolution in a multi-concurrency environment. Figure 5-9 shows how the DTM is positioned as a process across the architectural stack.

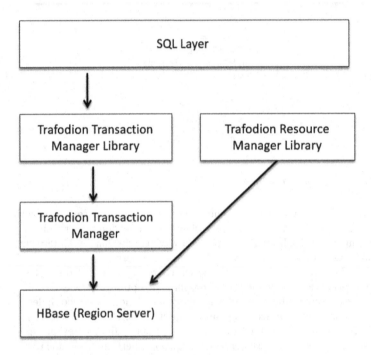

Figure 5-9. *Trafodion transactional management*

In the current version of DTM, the transaction endpoints are implemented within the HBase region servers as coprocessors (stored procedures, in the HBase world). Some portions of the DTM are written in C++, and it supports transaction recovery from a region server crash. An SQL call that is part of a transaction first goes through the Transaction Manager Library, which works in coordination with the Transaction Manager and Resource Manager Library. The Transaction Manager is the core of the DTM module.

For a given transaction with Begin/Commit and Abort semantics, the transaction first calls the Transaction Manager Library to put a fence around the regions that would be affected by the transaction. It generates a transaction ID and creates an internal transaction object and transaction state. This process also associates, or loops in, the HBase regions associated, which would eventually affect the data in those regions.

Also associated with the Transaction Manager (not shown in the figure above) is a transaction log. This log contains the metadata about the transaction and the information about the regions involved in the transaction. All updates that occur within the transaction boundaries are handled by the Resource Manager. It contains the core of the module that works with HBase tables to do the necessary scans to complete the get/put/delete-related work at the data level. All calls from either the Transaction Manager Library or the Resources Manager Library are coordinated with the corresponding HBase region servers.

Optimizations

Trafodion is a complex engine that provides many compile and runtime optimizations for operational workloads, both simple workloads accessing a single row of data to more complex OLTP transactions spanning multiple rows.

The executor process in Trafodion that executes the SQL queries is architected quite differently from most of the SQL-on-Hadoop engines. The executor process queries with data flowing entirely through memory and not hopping over disks, thus providing better performance by avoiding expensive I/O. The dataflow architecture of the executor processes leverages both partitioned parallelism, in which the operators all work on the same plan, or pipelined parallelism, whereby the architecture connects the operators in queues, with the output of one operator piped to the next operator, to execute the queries. Like most relational engines, it caches compiled SQL query plans for reuse and to avoid recompilations. It heavily leverages HBase filters and coprocessors and performs query fragment pushdown into the HBase engine wherever appropriate.

The executor process prepares two types of plans for most queries—parallel plans and non-parallel plans—and does a cost-based optimization on both to eventually use the one with lower cost. Internally, it is coded to use HBase APIs in the most optimized way, in terms of scan and data buffering and support for Rowset of data for large batches of rows. Trafodion optimizes the amount of data that is stored in HBase by using very small names for the column qualifiers and compression of the column names with right encoding. The executor process optimizes queries by using the right database statistics to identify and offset data skews. Internally, it implements parallel n-way joins and aggregation algorithms. (See Figure 5-10.)

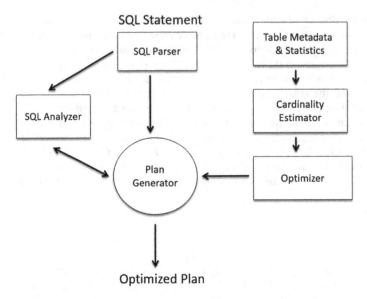

Figure 5-10. *View of Trafodion's query optimizer*

Apache Phoenix with HBase

Apache Phoenix is an SQL engine on top of HBase. Phoenix maps the HBase data model to the relational model. Phoenix can be used for building transactional systems on top of HBase for operational workloads using SQL. It is a lot like Trafodion but has better SQL support and coverage.

Apache Phoenix has the Query Engine, Metadata Repository, and JDBC Driver as its major architectural components. It supports composite keys on HBase and provides SQL data types on top of HBase's byte-oriented data with DDL-like schemas and definition syntax, very much like the relational world on top of data residing in HBase. It also provides read-only views on top of existing HBase data. New columns can be added at runtime to extend the schema. Phoenix supports all of the SQL join syntax with equality constraints and correlated subquery support over HBase. Phoenix can execute most of the TPC-H queries but does not support nested loop joins. The latest release of Phoenix has support for writing UDFs as well as support for extensive out-of-the-box built-in functions and transactions.

Transaction support is what is very essential to be used in OLTP workloads. Phoenix internally uses an open source framework called Tephra to provide support for transactional semantics. Out of the box, Phoenix supports Snapshot isolation, and the transactions can see their own uncommitted data and use optimistic concurrency control.

Apache Phoenix compiles SQL queries into a bunch of HBase scans and orchestrates execution of these scans to produce JDBC result sets. Phoenix stores its own metadata for each of the tables, columns, and data types in an HBase table. One of the main use cases of Apache Phoenix is to provide SQL access to HBase data. HBase data is difficult to access using its own command line interface (CLI) and proprietary scripting and Java APIs. Phoenix makes it extremely convenient to access HBase data using SQL and also applies its own set of optimizations and leverages to HBase's architecture to optimize the SQL queries and lower the latency.

Architecture

Phoenix compiles SQL queries into low-level HBase API calls. Phoenix is a lightweight process sitting on the region servers in HBase. It executes the HBase row scans in parallel.

Figure 5-11 shows the components of Phoenix with respect to HBase's components. The Phoenix JDBC driver is installed on the client side as jar files, while the Phoenix executable jar file is installed on the region servers in HBase.

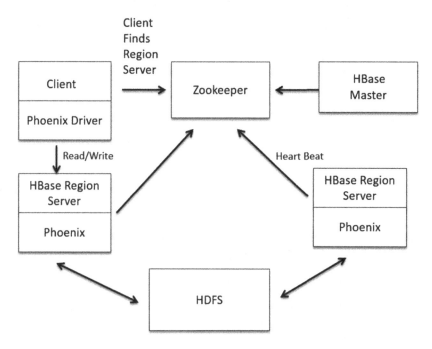

Figure 5-11. *Phoenix, with respect to HBase components*

The Phoenix client is part of the Phoenix query server, which is very similar to the HiveServer or HBase REST Server. It contains the JDBC and ODBC drivers for HBase. The Phoenix query engine is very typical of any SQL-based query engine and comprises a parser, query planner, and an optimizer, for which Phoenix uses Apache Calcite. Phoenix's query execution engine pushes as much compute to the HBase server as possible, leveraging the right hooks available in HBase API.

The Phoenix query engine stack is shown in Figure 5-12.

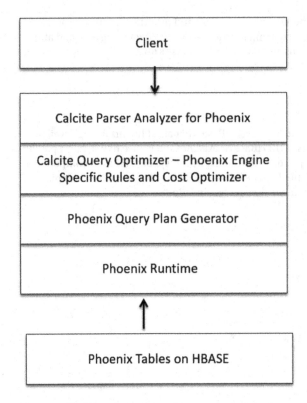

Figure 5-12. *Phoenix query engine component stack*

The Phoenix RPC endpoint contains the following components: the Dynamic Coprocessor and Dynamic Observers, as shown in Figure 5-13. Dynamic Coprocessors execute aggregation operations at each data node; the Dynamic Observers act as triggers to observe for events and sync data.

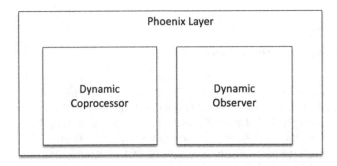

Figure 5-13. *Phoenix RPC endpoint*

Transaction Support in Phoenix

Figure 5-14 shows the overall high-level architectural components of Apache Phoenix that support transactions. Internally, Phoenix uses Apache Tephra, which provides globally consistent transactions on top of Apache HBase. HBase is by itself transactionally consistent at a single atomic row level. However, HBase has made some architectural trade-offs to not support global transaction across region servers and across tables over multiple rows. This support can be implemented in HBase using Apache Tephra. Figure 5-14 shows how Tephra integrates with HBase to provide global transactional support. We will not look into the internal details of Apache Tephra. Tephra internally uses HBase's native support for multiversioning, also known as multiversion concurrency control, abbreviated as MVCC or MCC, for transactional reads and writes. Each transaction sees its own "snapshot" of data, providing snapshot isolation of concurrent transactions out of the box.

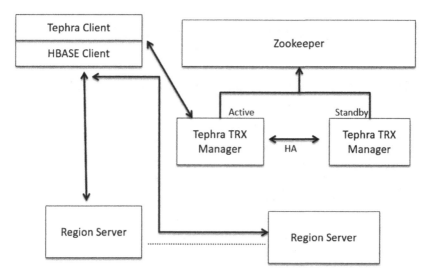

Figure 5-14. *Transaction Manager from Tephra within the HBase Phoenix ecosystem*

Internally, Phoenix uses the aforementioned architecture to support SQL transactions over HBase. Phoenix supports the REPEATABLE_READ isolation level by default.

Optimizations in Phoenix

Following are some of the most basic optimization techniques that Phoenix uses:

- It supports functional indexes and covered indexes, which are available on almost all RDBMS.

- It supports a statistics-driven parallel execution, whereby it can choose the smaller table for the build side during the join process.

- It offers query rewrite for correlated subqueries.

- It has predicate push down to the source data using HBase's rich filtering techniques and using its API.

Index Support

Phoenix has extensive support for indexes. Phoenix-generated indexes are stored as separate tables in HBase. Primary keys have to be specified during table creation time. Secondary indexes can be created by the usual CREATE INDEX DDL clause in Phoenix.

Three different secondary indexing strategies are supported by Apache Phoneix, based on usage patterns.

1. Immutable for write-once/append only data. This is managed by the Phoenix client-side code.

2. Global indexes for read-heavy and low-write mutable data. In this case, the actual data and index data could reside on separate servers. Server side intercepts the table updates and updates the indexes that would be on a remote server.

3. Local for write-heavy mutable or immutable data. In this case, the actual data and index data are co-located.

Apache Phoenix has its own set of limitations.

- Phoenix is not to be used if your use cases and the majority of your queries require sophisticated SQL queries that involve joins over large tables and use of advanced SQL queries.

- Do not use Phoenix if your queries require large scans, which cannot be avoided by indexes.

- It is advisable not to use Phoenix for ETL-related work, which involves large batches of data.

Kudu

In this section, we discuss Kudu, a relatively new storage engine in the Hadoop ecosystem. Kudu has been designed with the core idea that it can do both random updates and analytic workloads in the same storage, overcoming the operational problems of maintaining multiple systems for different types of workloads. Kudu is an open source storage engine for structured data that supports low-latency random access with efficient analytical access patterns. You can think of Kudu as an alternative to HDFS or HBase.

Kudu has been developed with two objectives in mind:

1. It makes management of streaming data for ad hoc analysis easier.

2. It bridges the gap from random access to update and append only mode of data operations, in other words, it covers the gap between a fast transactional store, at the same time providing storage for low-latency analytics.

From the preceding two points, it seems that Kudu is ideally suited for the middle ground. It is a system that can handle high volumes of reads/writes with high throughput and also provide the storage for low-latency analytic engines to work on. Kudu is not an analytic engine or a transactional engine.

Simply stated, it provides the storage capabilities that support both transactional workloads and analytical workloads, unlike HDFS, which was primarily meant for batch analytical workloads and read-only semantics. Kudu is, however, not an OLTP system, and it does not support transactional semantics or multi-row transactions.

So what problems does Kudu solve? In order to understand this, let's take a look at what an organization typically would do if it needed to support both transactional workloads and analytical workloads. In such cases, an organization would have one set of infrastructure, which would include storage and databases to support transactional workloads and another set of infrastructure for storage, and an analytic engine to support analytic workloads. These two infrastructures would have to be isolated from each other physically, so that they did not affect the SLAs of either.

With the advent of Kudu, the game changes. Now, the same organization can use Kudu to store both transactional and analytical data. Kudu provides strong performance for scan and random access and helps customers simplify complex hybrid architectures. It provides capabilities of updating data in place and avoids processing and data movement.

Kudu should not be confused with an in-memory database, file system, or SQL database, nor is it a replacement for HDFS or HBase. Single-row reads will be slower in Kudu than HBase, and, in addition, random updates in Kudu will be slower than with HBase. In the overall scheme of this, the picture below (Figure 5-15), taken from Cloudera, represents the positioning of Kudu, as compared to systems that do one thing well: either transactional or analytics.

Hadoop Storage Engines

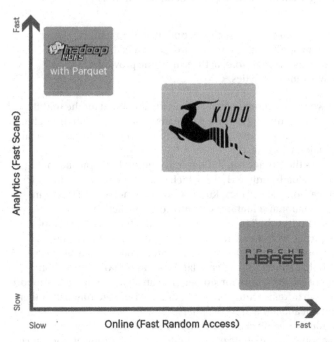

Figure 5-15. *Kudu positioned in comparison to transactional analytic systems*

Kudu Architecture

Kudu is a distributed system store for structured data. It is written in C++ and has no dependencies on other Hadoop components. It provides updateable storage, in which SQL operations support updates, deletes, and merges. However, Kudu does not have its own SQL interface. For analytic workloads, it has to be used with Impala/Vertica/Apache Drill for low-latency SQL. Kudu layers directly over the file system.

Kudu has a fixed table schema and uses column-oriented storage for disk and row-oriented storage for in-memory (which makes the updates easier to handle). In Kudu, tables must have a primary key, which is used for data sharding and provides access using this primary key.

In terms of performance optimizations, Kudu builds on the shoulders of giants and internally uses Bloom filters and lazy materialization of columnar data and the Raft consensus algorithm, to ensure consistency of the data.

Figure 5-16 shows where Kudu fits in the overall stack in the Hadoop ecosystem.

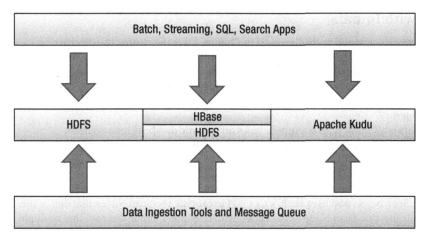

Figure 5-16. *Kudu and the Hadoop ecosystem stack*

In Kudu, tables are horizontally partitioned across nodes, and each such partition is called a tablet in Kudu speak. Each of these tablets has replicas that are kept in sync using the Raft consensus protocol. The architecture allows reading from any tablet, while all writes go to a master tablet. Each server on which a tablet exists is called a tablet server, and one tablet server can handle multiple tablets. Data is stored locally on the disk in each of these servers, and this is not HDFS. Each tablet can be typically 10s of GB, and a tablet server can hold up to about 100 tablets. Each of these tablets is replicated across other machines in the cluster for fault tolerance and reliability. Kudu has two types of partitioning strategies for distributing the data. Range partitioning, in which rows are distributed into tablets uses an ordered partitioning scheme, whereby each tablet contains a contiguous segment of the table's data. Hash partitioning distributes rows to tablets, based on the hash value of the row data.

Kudu has a master server that contains the metadata that describes the logical structure of the data stored in tablets. Multiple masters can be deployed to provide master failure reliability.

Updates in Kudu are handled using a log structured model (as in HBase), in which updates, deletes, upserts, and merges are buffered temporarily in memory before they are written to disk in columnar format.

Kudu Usage Scenarios

Kudu's inherent goal is to accept data very quickly and make that data available for analytics as soon as possible. Kudu has been built to accept lots of fast random writes from streams and also allows updates and inserts. Because of this, Kudu's main usage can be for low-latency analytics with an SQL engine—an alternative to Kafka.

Below, we outline in brief some of the use cases of Kudu.

125

Kudu with Impala

Impala, which was extensively discussed in Chapter 4, can work directly with Hive or files on HDFS. However, using Impala with Kudu offers several performance benefits. Kudu has been architected to deliver very high scan performance. Impala, an MPP engine, relies exclusively on high scan rates and file formats supporting that. Hence Kudu and Impala form a good combination for low-latency analytic query performance improvements.

Impala with Kudu is an attempt to build an analytic database management system into the Hadoop ecosystem. However, it is still very early for Kudu to claim this distinction.

During query processing, Impala fetches metadata from Kudu's master server, and during this process, defines the scan range. Impala defines a new processing node, called the Kudu Scan Node, and uses Kudu's C++ API to execute the Scan Nodes that define the scan. Typically, one Scan Node is associated with one tablet, but in the case that multiple Scan Nodes are associated with a tablet, Impala spawns multiple threads to scan in parallel.

Apart from the usual mechanics of scanning the data—data encoding in Parquet format, applying compression algorithms—Impala heavily relies on Kudu's capability to associate predicates with the scan, especially when the predicates are on the primary key. Impala relies on pushing the predicates down to the data storage layer, to optimize both the I/O and improve scan performance.

Kudu As an Alternative to Kafka

Kudu can be thought of as a more flexible and reliable queueing system, like Kafka, or, in other words, a publish/subscribe system based on a database. Kudu overcomes some of the architectural- and usability-related trade-offs for throughput that Kafka made. Use cases such as modifying the queue after en-queuing and a queue per user, are difficult to do in Kafka, and Kudu's is architected to overcome these problems.

Kudu ensures consistency, unlike Kafka, which relies on an asynchronous replication system. Kudu has been architected to satisfy reads and writes within a bounded interval and guarantees a consistent view of the data, using the Raft consensus protocol.

Another tool that has recently been open sourced to address operational workloads on big data systems is Splice Machines. We will not be covering this tool in this book.

Summary

This chapter extensively covered SQL engines, which span the gamut of applications, from being used for processing semi-structured data to stream processing and usage in operational systems with transactional support. This field is a rapidly developing one, with new products being created with newer ideas and innovations.

In the next chapter, we will cover the new and exciting innovations occurring in the world of SQL engines on big data, in which totally new concepts and ways of solving SQL with big data are addressed.

Innovations and the Road Ahead

This is an exciting chapter that discusses the shiny new products and tools addressing SQL on Hadoop that are evolving in the market. It discusses the new concept of hybrid transaction/analytical processing (HTAP), which addresses consolidation of online transaction processing (OLTP) and online analytical processing (OLAP) platforms. This chapter considers these at a high level and from an architecture perspective. These products are in a state of evolution and rapid change and must to be tested further in actual production systems.

BlinkDB

In this section, we will look at an interesting SQL engine called BlinkDB. BlinkDB was innovated in the same research lab as Spark—AMPLabs. BlinkDB is an approximate interactive, in-memory SQL engine for large data sets.

With many projects, there is a classic perception that one can realize any two of three objectives (refer to Figure 6-1), as most project managers would have it. In fact, no project can accomplish all three objectives at the same time.

Figure 6-1. *Choose any two features for a project. You cannot have all three*

© Sumit Pal 2016

S. Pal, *SQL on Big Data*, DOI 10.1007/978-1-4842-2247-8_6

BlinkDB follows the same concept. Any SQL engine for big data processing can have any two of the desired features, but not all three at once, as shown in Figure 6-2.

Figure 6-2. *Choose any two features for an SQL engine. You cannot have all three*

In order to improve performance and lower latency of SQL queries on large data sets, BlinkDB decided to get rid of accuracy, within an error threshold or margin. In the real world, especially in analytics, which is not accounting, we can afford to be slightly off a correct/accurate/precise number by a certain margin.

For example, when counting the number of visitors to a web site, it is fine if the actual number is something like 245,885 in the last 24 hours and your query returns a result of 240,000, but returns it fast—let's say, in 1 second rather than waiting for 30 seconds to get a more accurate number. This is what BlinkDB excels in: it provides a massive boost to the latency by arriving at a result in a much shorter time, with the returned result within a specific error range.

As shown in Figure 6-3, the basic idea of BlinkDB is to return results faster with low latency within a given threshold. As the threshold approaches zero, or as the result approaches higher levels of accuracy, the execution time increases.

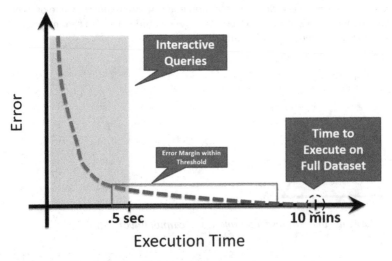

Figure 6-3. *Varying execution times with error rate*

BlinkDB is based on deep math and statistics and a lot of probability theory as a core part of its engine. The core part of BlinkDB is the right data sampling, so that during runtime, the queries are only executed on the sampled data, but the magic is that it still returns the results within the error margin, but with a much lower latency.

How Does It Work

BlinkDB is an SQL engine that uses a variety of random and stratified data samples from an original data set. At runtime, it executes the SQL queries on these data samples. The magic of the query engine lies in how it selects the sampled data.

In the world of data sampling, there are primarily two ways of sampling data

1. *Uniform Sampling*

2. *Stratified Sampling.* Stratified sampling is the process of choosing a random sample in which members of the population are divided into strata/groups/clusters and then samples are randomly selected from the clusters.

Queries

BlinkDB offers a variant of the well-known SQL syntax whereby one can make analytic queries that return within a specific time or return results with an error rate and confidence interval that is user-specified.

```
SELECT avg (sessionTime) FROM Table WHERE city='Boston' WITHIN .1 SECONDS
SELECT avg (sessionTime) FROM Table WHERE city='Boston' ERROR 0.1 CONFIDENCE
99.0%
```

BlinkDB also adds new predefined UDFs, based on approximate aggregate functions with statistical closed forms, to HiveQL: approx_avg(), approx_sum(), approx_count().

Data Sample Management

When BlinkDB starts and is given a data set, it creates an optimal set of samples on native data sets and summarized views based on query history and workload characteristics that the data set will cater to. This process is shown in Figure 6-4.

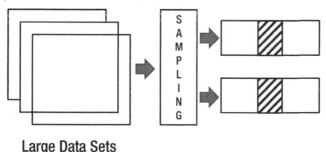

Large Data Sets

Figure 6-4. *Sampling a data set for best results*

Once the samples are created, they can be stored on disk or cached in memory, with optimized data formats for faster execution, loading, and efficient storage. These samples can be created either with no known training or information as to the type of query patterns, or BlinkDB can be configured to generate these samples, based on some of the typical queries that the engine will be handling at runtime, as shown in Figure 6-5.

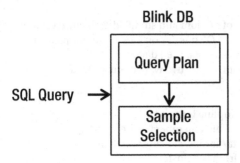

Figure 6-5. *Query is executed on the samples pre-prepared by BlinkDB*

Execution

When a given query is sent to the BlinkDB engine, it picks up the best sample out of the pre-created samples, based on query latency and accuracy requirements desired by the end user, and executes the query on that sample, to return query results with low latency.

GPU Is the New CPU—SQL Engines Based on GPUs

In this section, we will explore some upcoming SQL engines on big data that leverage GPUs to do blazing fast computations. These engines leverage the parallel power of modern GPUs and try to bring in a lag-free data exploration experience on large data sets.

From being used mainly in the high-resolution graphics engines in the gaming industry, graphics processing units (GPUs) are rapidly evolving to become the main computation engine in virtual reality (VR) engines, self-driving vehicles, drones, and machine learning. GPUs have also found a new home with their introduction into the computing brain of next generation analytic engines.

Figure 6-6 shows the difference, from an architectural perspective, in the layout of cores for GPUs as compared to CPUs.

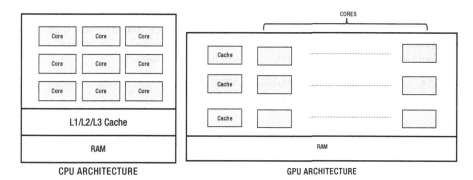

Figure 6-6. Architectural differences between GPUs and CPUs, based on core layouts

MapD (Massively Parallel Database)

MapD is a GPU-powered database and visual analytics platform using GPUs that provides interactive exploration on extremely large data sets with very low latency. MapD leverages GPUs to execute SQL queries in parallel across nearly 40K cores per server, yielding massive speedups over other SQL engines. It also leverages graphic processing capabilities to provide data visualization and visual insights into complex data sets.

MapD is a full-blown product that offers a high-speed SQL-compatible database that internally leverages columnar data storage and processing formats and a data visualization front end to drive real-time decision making. MapD doesn't require GPUs and can run on CPUs, but the architecture is tuned for massively parallel computation, and the performance on GPUs is an order of magnitude better than on CPUs with multiple cores and threads per core.

GPUs perform best on algorithms that can be parallelized with the least amount of branching in algorithms that leverage each core to do the same operation repeatedly. One of the best things about GPU-based computes is that, when GPUs are used for query execution, the CPU is not doing anything, and its compute capacity can be used to perform other tasks associated with the query execution.

MapD leverages three major traits of GPUs to build a scalable system that allows high-speed SQL querying, advanced analytics, and data visualization—all in one system.

1. Computational parallelism

2. High-speed memory

3. Graphics pipeline

Currently, MapD is only architected to be deployed on a single node with up to eight of Nvidia's top-of-the-line Tesla K80 coprocessors; however, work is under way to make it a distributed database. Like Impala and Spark SQL, MapD also uses LLVM to generate and compile SQL code on the fly for massive speedup. It is written in C++ and leverages CUDA and OpenCL to talk to the GPUs.

Internally, MapD uses a columnar data store and uses data compression to make memory on the GPUs perform better. It offers connectivity to the outside world, using both JDBC/ODBC and Thrift servers.

Some of the distinguishing features of MapD include the following:

- Caching hot data in the GPU memory

- Vectorizing the queries like other SQL engines we have seen to leverage parallelism

- Built-in kernel operators for frequently used database operations, to reduce the delay in code generation on the fly, because GPU code generation takes more time than typical CPU code generation

- Routine leveraging of both the GPU and CPU when a data set cannot fit into GPUs

- Very deep built-in text mining features

With all the preceding features and capabilities, MapD can support a scan rate of almost 2-3TB/sec of data, which is 40 times faster than similarly configured CPU servers.

As GPUs performance and memory capabilities improve further, MapD has a roadmap to utilize the next generation GPUs to optimize its performance. One of the main problems of GPU-based databases is the low limited size of the memory on the GPU. However, Nvidia's roadmap to couple GPUs more tightly with the CPUs using NVlink ports and use of InfiniBand network cards can change all that. InfiniBand network can also help with distributed join-based queries that can require a large amount of data shuffling.

Architecture of MapD

A very high-level overview of MapD architecture is shown in Figure 6-7. It has ODBC and Thrift connectors to allow third- party tools and libraries to connect to the engine and execute SQL queries. The MapD engine not only processes SQL queries but also provides the native graphic rendering capabilities to show high-resolution images for large-scale data visualization.

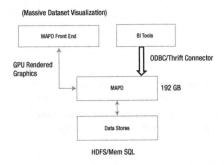

Figure 6-7. *High-level MapD architecture*

GPUdb

MapD, however, is not a distributed SQL engine. Currently, it is designed to work on a stand-alone machine. A close open source competitor to MapD is GPUdb, which is a distributed database with SQL capabilities. GPUdb provides ODBC connectors and an API for developers and business analysts to interact with and provides standard SQL interface to interact with the database. It provides ANSI SQL '92 compatible SQL interface and also has a RESTful API.

GPUdb leverages many-core devices and is currently supported with NVIDIA GPUs and Xeon Phi many-core devices. It works a lot like an MPP engine, wherein the core engine is deployed on each node in the cluster, preferably with identical nodes and same number of GPUs. A single node is chosen to be the coordination/aggregation node. The cluster can be scaled up or down, depending on the storage and query efficiency requirements.

SQream

Another analytic SQL engine database based on GPUs is SQream. SQream uses MPP on chip technology to deliver power of more than 10K cores for high-performance computing in a single appliance.

SQream DB is a massively parallel analytic database SQL engine using GPUs to harness its unique performance characteristics for handling large-scale data sets. It runs on single or multiple NVIDIA GPUs. It supports ANSI SQL. SQream provides JDBC and ODBC interfaces for ETL and BI tools to be easily connected.

Internally, SQream is a columnar database in which each column is stored as a collection of data chunks. SQream creates its own metadata on top of each column, which results in smarter and faster access to large data sets. (See Figure 6-8.)

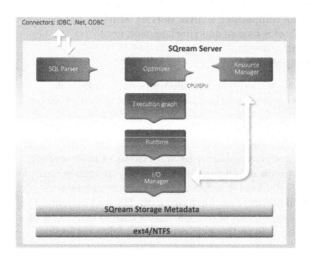

Figure 6-8. *High-level SQream architecture (courtesy of SQream Technologies)*

SQream works by transforming SQL queries into parallelizable relational algebra query fragments. Like any other SQL engine, SQream's query optimizer does a lot of the hard work in the background, to optimize the queries, optimize the I/O workload, and effectively utilize the massive parallelism offered by the GPUs. The execution plan chosen by the optimizer is the one that is optimized for the GPUs, based on the GPU architecture and chipsets used. SQream's storage and query engines are both columnar, and, to process the data, the query engine does not have to convert the compressed columnar data format back to the uncompressed row format. This makes SQream faster than a lot of the other columnar analytic databases out there, in terms of performance, scalability, and concurrency. Using compression results in lower I/O, and because of the GPUs' processing capabilities, decompression, if and when needed, is massively faster, as compared to when running on CPU-based machines.

During data ingestion, all the metadata is generated by the SQream's ingestor process, which helps the query engine to build the optimized query plans.

Apache Kylin

Online analytical processing (OLAP), which was so popular in the last decade of the last century and the first decade of this century and beyond, got sidelined by the big data tools expansion, but it is making a comeback, by reinventing itself for the world of big data. There were two reasons why OLAP became so popular.

1. As data sets were growing in size and relational databases were becoming bloated and slow in query response, especially for analytical queries, database engineers invented the concepts of OLAP and cubes to perform analytical queries with lower latency.

2. It provided the right data structures to do multidimensional querying, especially for complicated analytic queries, with each OLAP provider having its own querying language, until providers came up with a standard language called MDX (Multidimensional Expressions).

One of the reasons OLAP slowly started losing its value, especially as data sets started getting bigger and queries became more complex, was because OLAP relied on building either one right cube that could address almost all the queries or multiple cubes, a combination of which could support most of the query workloads. Building cubes consumed a lot of time, resources, storage, and maintenance work during the ETL stage. This often entailed the possibilities of missing out on the SLAs. However, more recently, two new OLAP engines on Hadoop with an SQL interface (not MDX) are gaining traction in the world of big data for doing SQL-based analytics. Apache Kylin, an open source project started in South Korea, and AtScale, a startup based in the Silicon Valley, are trying to innovate and build OLAP engines for big data, using the current tools in the big data ecosystem. We discuss Apache Kylin and its architecture in the following sections.

Kylin is an open source distributed analytics engine that provides SQL interface and OLAP capabilities on Hadoop for large data sets. Kylin has been designed to reduce query latency on Hadoop and provide interactive SQL analysis on Hadoop. This allows Kylin to be integrated well with BI and third-party tools. Internally, Kylin is a MOLAP engine (multidimensional OLAP engine), in which the data is precomputed along different dimensions of interest and stored as pre-built and precomputed cubes. MOLAP is much faster but is inflexible and requires the cubes to be refreshed as data changes. The other type of OLAP is ROLAP (relational OLAP), as used in star or snow-flake schemas in data warehouses to do runtime aggregation. ROLAP is flexible but much slower. All existing SQL-on-Hadoop engines can be classified as ROLAP engines.

Kylin builds data cubes (MOLAP) from an underlying Hive table (ROLAP), according to the metadata specification. When an SQL query comes into Kylin, if the query can be fulfilled by an existing pre-built data cube, Kylin routes the query to the data cube and delivers the results immediately. These precomputed data cubes reside in HBase. If the query can't be fulfilled by an existing cube, Kylin will route the query to the Hive table that is ROLAP and trigger a cube-building process for the query, so that future queries can be supported by the cube.

Apart from a more general set of features, Kylin also provides the following enterprise-level features out of the box:

- Incremental refresh of cubes

- A web interface to manage, build, monitor, and query cubes

- Under-the-covers leverage HBase for query latency

- Approximate query capabilities for distinct count performance, using the HyperLogLog algorithm

- Compression and encoding Support

- Job management and monitoring

- LDAP integration

Figure 6-9 and Figure 6-10 provide a high-level overview of the internals of Apache Kylin and how it works.

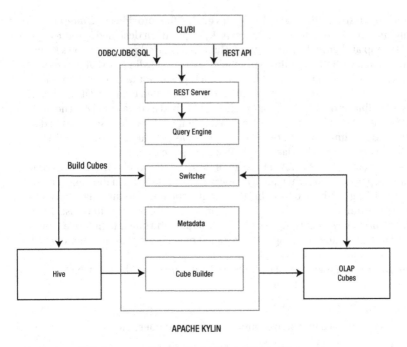

Figure 6-9. *Kylin's process flow for executing a SQL query*

Kylin is fronted by a REST server, which accepts SQL queries from third-party tools. On receiving a query, the REST server hands over the SQL query to the query engine, which decides the optimal way to execute the query. This optimization can be for either the MapReduce-based job for building the cube to satisfy the query or for running the query on an already built data cube that resides in HBase.

Kylin maintains two types of Metadata: end-user Metadata, which forms the data model for the star schema, and metadata for the cubes that have been generated by Kylin and stored in HBase.

Cubes are built using MapReduce, and, hence, this can be a time-consuming process. Typically, this process would be baked in as part of the ETL pipeline, so that the cube is ready to be queried when queries arrive in real time. In case a cube has not been built for a specific SQL query, and the already built cubes in HBase cannot satisfy the query, i.e, do not have the data for the query, Kylin offloads the cube-building process by running a MapReduce job on Hive for building the new cube. This new cube is then moved to HBase, the query results are executed on HBase, and the results are returned. The latter workflow can result in significant delays in query latency.

Kylin uses HBase as the storage engine and leverages the HBase coprocessor to reduce network traffic, parallelize scan logic, and improve the latency of the queries.

As seen in Figure 6-10, – Apache Calcite is used internally by Kylin as the SQL query optimization engine which that optimizes the query before it is executed either by the MapReduce job in Hive or within the pre-built cube in HBase.

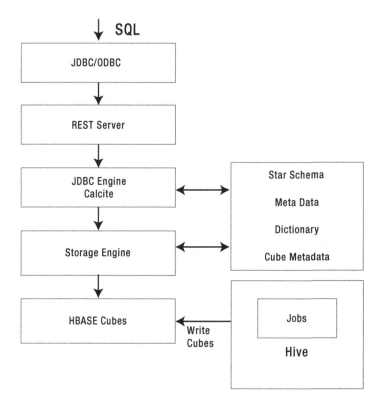

Figure 6-10. Kylin high-level architecture

Apache Lens

Apache Lens is a project that tries to abstract out data silos, by providing a single view of data across different data stores. It also tries to provide an optimal execution environment for the analytical queries across all the data silos it abstracts out. It tries to achieve a unified view of the data source across either Hadoop-based systems or data warehouses, by providing a uniform metadata layer.

An approximate architecture is shown in Figure 6-11. Apache Lens has been designed with a pluggable architecture in mind. Modules for data access and processing engines can be plugged in to the overall architecture of Apache Lens. Apache Lens supports an OLAP-based data model across all the data stores. It also supports an SQL interface on top of it that can be accessed using a REST interface. Internally, Apache Lens models all the tables as facts and dimensions, and all its data-management functions are modeled along the lines of an OLAP model.

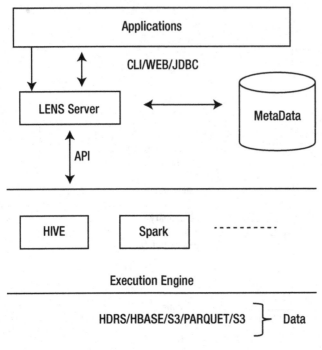

Figure 6-11. *Apache Lens server—how it fits into the overall data pipeline*

It supports a high-level SQL-like query language to describe data sets organized as cubes. CLI-based and third-party-tools-based queries are issued through Java Database Connectivity (JDBC) libraries.

An application server hosts the REST server, which is the gateway for ad hoc and metadata queries. It also has a cost-based optimized engine that selects the best execution engine for a given query, based on the query cost.

It runs a REST-based server—Lens Server—which has several endpoints for each type of service. It has endpoints for the following types of services across all the data stores it abstracts: Metadata Service, Query Service, Session Service, and Scheduler Service.

> *Metadata Service*: This provides an abstract metadata view over tiered data stores, which provides a uniform layer for data flow and data pipelines to share and access the metadata across the silos. Any DDL-related operations are handled by this service.

> *Query Service*: This is used to run queries across different data stores that have been configured. Internally, it uses a database resource service, which automatically adds jar files at runtime, based on the query destination. Internally, the query service uses the session service to create a session to the data store to which the query is directed. It also monitors the queries, returns the results, and tracks the query history across the different data stores.

Session Service: All session-level operations are performed using REST and Java APIs. Sessions allows configurations to be set across a group of queries. Any metadata operation or database query operation must use Session Service.

Apache Tajo

Apache Tajo, an open source project since 2014, is a distributed data-processing framework that does not use MapReduce and has an SQL interface. Tajo is designed for low-latency ad hoc queries and ETL on large data sets stored on HDFS and/or other data sources. Its goal is to provide a single framework that can be used both for ETL (long-running batch processing) as well as for interactive ad hoc queries.

Tajo is a data-warehouse system with ANSI SQL compliance. It is built as a master/slave architecture with a single master and multiple workers and looks strikingly similar to Hive. The master is the gateway to the framework for clients. It also coordinates query processing across the slaves on the cluster. The master also performs resource tracking and allocation across the cluster, while the slaves run in a cluster and process the data stored on the local nodes.

An SQL query goes through the same layers of analysis and planning, to generate the logical and optimized physical plan with the data flow. Tajo provides query federation across multiple data silos residing in NoSQL, RDBMS, or Cloud or on-premise across multiple formats, such as Parquet, JSON, Avro, ORC, CSV, and it offers index and UDAF support.

Tajo has a pluggable storage framework that can connect to most of the data sources available today. It also has its own query optimizer, which is a combination of rule-based and cost-based optimizer. Figure 6-12 provides a high-level overview of Apache Tajo architecture.

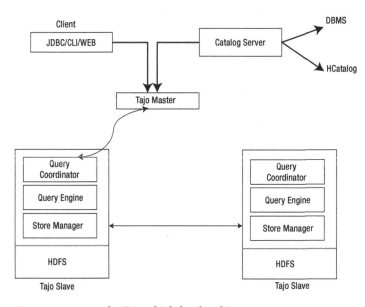

Figure 6-12. *Apache Tajo—high-level architecture*

During query execution, Tajo can exploit the processing capabilities and optimizations built into the underlying storage or data store. For query federation, Tajo has to have a global view of the metadata across different storages. Tajo maintains its own metadata and also references the metadata for each of the data stores it is querying in the federated query. SQL query federation is shown in Figure 6-13.

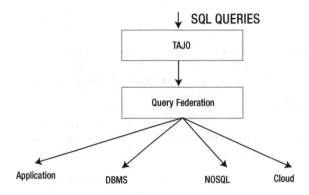

Figure 6-13. *Query federation in Apache Tajo*

HTAP

In this section we will briefly try to cover and explain what this new term coined by Gartner in 2014 is all about and how SQL on big data is helping this vision to come true in light of HTAP.

HTAP stands for *Hybrid Transactional/Analytical Processing*. This term is more applicable to enterprises. In a traditional enterprise, there is a set of database processing systems that keep the operational applications running for the enterprise's functional capabilities. These database processing systems are mostly transactional and are always supposed to be on, with strict SLAs, and can process data in real time.

On the other side is a set of database processing systems, for analytics, BI, reporting, and data warehousing, where batch processing such as ETL is done. The data for analytics primarily comes from operational data. OLTP and operational data systems are essential to keeping the business operating, while analytics and BI help to improve business. Figure 6-14 offers a high-level overview of these systems.

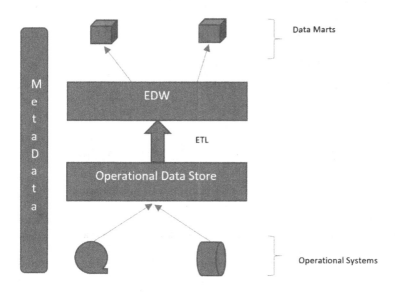

Figure 6-14. *Operational data store and EDWs*

Traditionally, these different silos of data-processing tools, frameworks, and databases are installed on different hardware, may be located in different data centers, and require totally different skill sets, from development and maintenance perspectives. This sort of fragmented system causes multiple problems.

- Different systems have to be kept operational, which in itself is a huge challenge.

- There are huge delays in performing analytics, because data from operational systems has to be moved to the data warehouses for analytics.

- Multiple investments, in terms of licensing for different technologies, each of which is suited for a specific purpose, are required.

Today, businesses demand immediate analytics, data-driven decision making. The old approach of delivering analytics through a layered architecture is no longer sufficient. Today's business managers and analysts want to follow up-to-the-minute changes and fluctuations in the operational aspects of their businesses. For example, recommendation algorithms for retailers must use up-to-date information on purchases by similar users, in order to recommend new products to other users with similar tastes. Digital advertisers seek to improve their targeting algorithms with up-to-the-minute clickstream data.

The idea of HTAP is to provide a unified system in which end users do not have to use different systems—for storage or for differing workloads—whether they want to use current or historical data. This implied creation of a combined operational and analytical environment is called HTAP.

The challenges of building an HTAP system are numerous.

- A single query engine for all workloads

- Support for multiple storage engines

- The same data model for all workloads

- Enterprise-grade features—security, failover, backup, and concurrency

The biggest challenge of HTAP is to have a single query engine that works across all workloads and across multiple storage systems. The query engine should allow the client to submit queries and get the results, as well as compile, optimize, and execute the query. The query engine has to support clustering, partitioning, and transaction support (along with support from the storage engine, for transactions). An HTAP system would also have to work across multiple storage engines, because, typically, HTAP systems have to support both transactional (write-heavy, with large concurrency) workloads, as well as analytic queries (read-heavy) workloads with multiple different data formats. Figure 6-15 illustrates this idea.

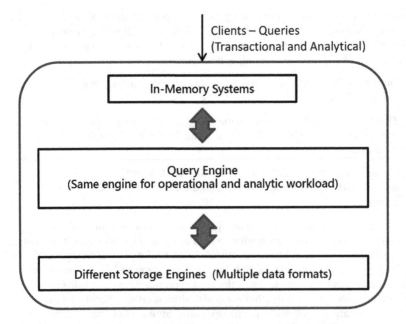

Figure 6-15. *What the HTAP high-level architecture might look like*

There are two fundamental forces happening in today's technology that can make the HTAP vision a reality:

1. *In-memory systems*: These avoid disk-based systems and provide the latency SLAs.

2. *Scale-out architectures*: Traditionally, it has been difficult to scale out relational databases; however, with changes to underlying architectures in new engines, starting from Google's F1 engine to newer and commercial ones such as MemSQL, NuoDB, and VoltDB, for example, building distributed OLTP systems that can scale out has become a reality.

Advantages of HTAP

Listed below are some of the advantages of an HTAP system.

- It simplifies data transfer.

- Analytics can rely upon the freshest data.

- It reduces ETL and pipeline complexity.

- There is no need to pre-aggregate, requiring fewer systems.

HTAP can perform time-sensitive transactional and analytical operations in a single database system. This reduces costs and administrative and operational overhead. With HTAP, no data movement is required from operational databases to data warehouses or data marts for analytics. Data is processed in a single system, eliminating ETL.

Figure 6-16 illustrates what is essentially possible with HTAP.

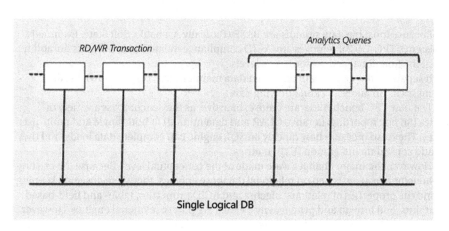

Figure 6-16. *Single DB for both distributed transactions and analytics*

With all the advances occurring in the world of databases, HTAP tries essentially to bring in a single query engine for all workloads, whether they are OLTP or OLAP workloads.

With the rapid evolution of new classes of database engines called NewSQL—VoltDB, NuoDB, and Trafodion (covered in Chapter 5) being the primary forerunners in this space—it seems that HTAP is on the verge of possibly providing what could be termed database nirvana.

TPC Benchmark

Until about the beginning of 2016, most of the SQL-on-Hadoop engine vendors were running SQL queries to do the benchmarking for their SQL queries. The problem was that those sets of 50–100 queries were designed for relational databases, and big data vendors were somehow trying to shoehorn those queries into their engines and comparing the results. Also, vendors were cherry-picking parts of the TPC-DS Benchmark to give a skewed picture of their engine capabilities. This resulted in skewed interpretations of those queries, as they applied to the SQL-on-Hadoop engines.

Recently, the Transaction Processing Performance Council (TPC) designed a new set of queries and metrics. They represent a variation on the long-standing TPC-DS Benchmark and resulted in a newer version called TPC-DS 2.0. TPC-DS 2.0 is the first industry standard benchmark for measuring the end-to-end performance of SQL engines in the big data space. The latest version of TPC-DS made the following changes to the 1.0 version:

- It increases the minimum raw data set size to 1TB, with a ceiling of 100TB.

- It eliminates benchmarking of update statements on dimension tables.

Because most big data systems are BASE (Basically Available, Soft State, Eventually consistent), TPC-DS 2.0 removes any ACID compliance–related tests but adds durability tests at the functional and performance levels.

It separates the querying of data from data maintenance, because most big data systems focus on analyzing and querying data.

The new TPC benchmarks are quite exhaustive, as they encompass a variety of queries (ad hoc reporting, iterative OLAP, and data mining) in both single and multi-user modes. They also measure how quickly an SQL engine can complete data loads, and they also add some data integration (ETL) metrics.

However, the major changes were made at the conceptual level. Because the existing TPC benchmarks were based on relational database engines, they were designed keeping in mind the properties of relational algebra and ACID properties, table- and field-based constraints, and foreign and primary keys, which are part of relational engines. However, in the brave new world of big data, none of these constraints or ACID capabilities applies.

The new benchmarks give customers better clarity for comparing SQL execution engines and query optimizer capabilities. Also, some changes have been made concerning how the final score, in terms of performance, is determined in the new TPC-Benchmark. In the previous TPC version, various subcomponents were weighted more or less equally, by calculating the mean across all the components. However, in the latest version of the TPC-Benchmark on big data, the calculations use a geometric mean.

With the proliferation of big data systems being deployed using VMs or container-based solutions on the cloud, the new benchmarks accommodate performance for virtualized environments as well. This benchmark is known as TPCx-V. This virtualized TPC measurement can offer good concrete metrics with which to evaluate and compare virtualized environments for production systems.

Vendors will be adapting to the new TPC-Benchmark soon and, based on their usage and results, some changes will result in a tweak of the TPC-Benchmark, to accord with current usage.

Summary

This chapter is the last in the book, and it completes our journey through the different technologies and architectures that go into building an SQL engine on a big data platform.

This chapter provided a bird's-eye view of what is happening in the brave new world of SQL on big data and how research labs and organizations are innovating with new ideas, concepts, and approaches to solving problems. This is an area of frantic activity and fierce competition, and things will keep changing and evolving in this space with the adoption of new technologies and new, innovative ideas.

Appendix

This appendix highlights four items that summarize the most important topics covered in this book.

Figure A-1 is a mind map that summarizes the different SQL engine solutions, based on their applicability and capabilities, consolidated in a single diagram. However, please keep in mind that with rapid changes to technology and new solutions coming to market, this map is bound to change over time.

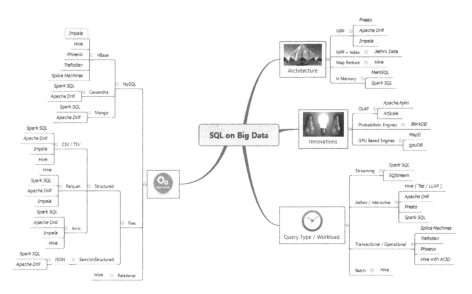

Figure A-1. *SQL on big data choices*

Figure A-2 shows the current SQL engine technology solutions available on the market for developing operational systems and performing operational analytics with big data.

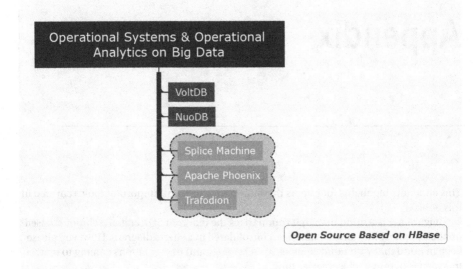

Figure A-2. *Operational SQL engines—choices*

Table A-1 summarizes the features and characteristics to support operational systems and operational analytics that one should look for in an SQL engine.

Table A-1. *Characteristics to Look for Before Making a Decision Regarding Operational SQL Engines*

Features	Apache Phoenix	Trafodion	VoltDB	NuoDB	SpliceMachine
ACID Support					
Adding New Columns					
Latency • Worst Case • Average Case • Best Case					
Concurrency • (10–100 Users) • (100–1K Users) • (1K+ Users)					
Failover					
High Availability					
Additional Nodes					

(continued)

Table A-1. (*continued*)

Features	Apache Phoenix	Trafodion	VoltDB	NuoDB	SpliceMachine
Scalability					
Hardware Requirement Commodity High-End Servers High-Memory Servers					
Cluster Size Limitations					
Licensing					
Replication					
CAP Characteristic					
Security Features					
Data Sources Support					
Storage Format Support					
Compression					
Hadoop Distros Support					
Data Balancing					
Tool Support Admin Monitoring Troubleshooting Performance Measurement					
Upgrades Downtime Migration of Schema					
Data Partitioning Strategies					
Query Troubleshooting Capabilities Explain Plan Plan Caching Query Result Caching					
Data-Mining Algorithms					
Search Capabilities— Integration Solr/ ElasticSearch					

Table A-2 summarizes the features and characteristics to support low-latency interactive ad hoc SQL queries that one should look for in an SQL engine.

Table A-2. *Characteristics to Look for Before Making a Decision Regarding Interactive SQL Engines*

Features	Apache Drill	Impala	Spark SQL	Vertica	Jethro
Latency • Worst Case • Average Case • Best Case • Low Data Set Size (100GB) • Medium Data Set Size (100GB-10TB) • Huge Data Set Size (>10TB)					
Concurrency • (10–100 Users) • (100–1K Users) • (1K+ Users)					
Failover					
High Availability					
Additional Nodes					
Scalability					
Hardware Requirement • Commodity • High-End Servers • High-Memory Servers					
Cluster Size Limitations					
Licensing					
Replication					
CAP characteristic					
UDF Support					
SQL Support					
Security Features • Access (Row, Column) • Encryption (Rest, Motion)					

(continued)

Table A-2. (*continued*)

Features	Apache Drill	Impala	Spark SQL	Vertica	Jethro
Data Sources Support • HDFS • S3					
Storage Format Support • Parquet • ORC • Avro • Text • Un-structured • JSON • SequenceFile					
Compression • Zlib • Gzip • BZIP • Snappy • LZO					
Hadoop Distro Support • MapR • Cloudera • HDP					
Data Balancing					
Tool Support • Admin • Monitoring • Troubleshooting • Performance Measurement					
SPOF					
Data-Ingestion Tools					
Customer Base					
Pricing Model • Data Size • Number of Nodes					
• Upgrades • Downtime • Migration of Schema					

(*continued*)

Table A-2. (*continued*)

Features	Apache Drill	Impala	Spark SQL	Vertica	Jethro
Data-Partitioning Strategies					
• Query Troubleshooting Capabilities • Explain Plan • Plan Caching • Query Result Caching					
Data Mining Algorithms					
Search Capabilities • Integration Solr/ ElasticSearch					

Index

Get the eBook for only $4.99!

Why limit yourself?

Now you can take the weightless companion with you wherever you go and access your content on your PC, phone, tablet, or reader.

Since you've purchased this print book, we are happy to offer you the eBook for just $4.99.

Convenient and fully searchable, the PDF version enables you to easily find and copy code—or perform examples by quickly toggling between instructions and applications.

To learn more, go to http://www.apress.com/us/shop/companion or contact support@apress.com.

Printed in the United States
By Bookmasters